decorating easy

DECORATING
easy

Create a simple,
comfortable home with
pure style

Jane Cumberbatch

QUADRILLE

SPECIAL PHOTOGRAPHY BY JENNY ZARINS

ILLUSTRATIONS BY KATE STORER

*For Alastair, Tom,
Georgie and Gracie*

Editorial Director Jane O'Shea
Creative Director Helen Lewis
Project Editor Lisa Pendreigh
Designer Lawrence Morton
Photographer Jenny Zarins
Illustrator Kate Storer
Styling Assistant Charlotte Kennedy-Cochran-Patrick
Production Director Vincent Smith
Production Controller Ruth Deary

First published in 2005 by Quadrille Publishing Ltd,
Alhambra House, 27–31 Charing Cross Road, London WC2H 0LS

Cataloguing in Publication Data: a record of this book is
available from the British Library.

ISBN 1 84400 197 0

Printed in Singapore

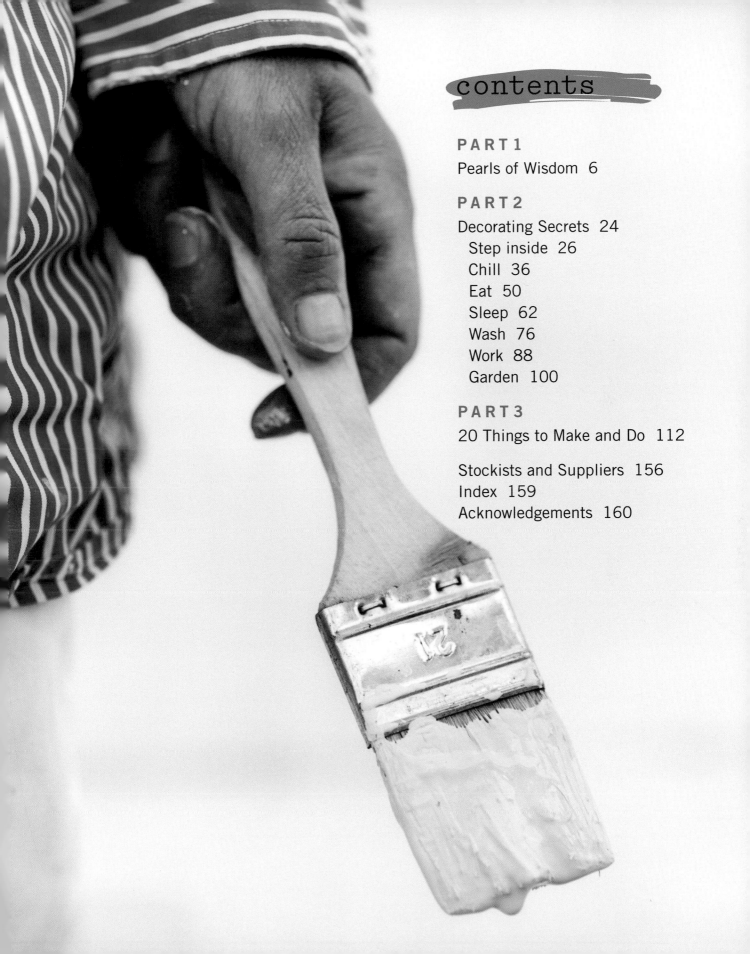

contents

PART 1

Pearls of wisdom

down to earth

USE SIMPLE IDEAS AND FLEXIBLE THINKING TO MAKE YOUR HOME A HAVEN FROM THE STRESSES AND STRAINS OF DAILY LIFE.

Decorating Easy is about making your home comfortable and modern without spending a fortune. My ideas will hopefully enable you to create a stylish space on a budget, without forsaking looks and function. *Decorating Easy* is not about having a glossy show house – increasingly the home has become the ultimate trophy, something to show off rather than a domestic necessity. It is rather more down to earth (more earthy than earnest) and more in tune with real life and its imperfections than the glossy airbrushed interiors that advertisers seduce use into believing we should aspire to.

Decorating Easy is making the best of what you've got, and thinking in a more resourceful, and, wherever possible a more eco-conscious way. It is about paring down and living with less to keep your life more in control. And it is also about learning to be elastic in your planning and thinking, so your aims and needs are more likely to be realised.

decorating easy means:

✳ writing down your list of priorities: getting the big jobs done first, such as electrics and plumbing

✳ doing as much as you can yourself

✳ reviving a tired interior with fresh coats of your favourite paint

✳ not hankering after fancy fitted kitchens, trendy sofas and so on (otherwise your budget will soon become a teeny weeny one); basic designs can look just as good

✳ shopping in ordinary stores for cheap, functional but good-looking objects: candles, bowls, good brooms and so on

✳ waiting for the sales to chase bargains in linen sheets, cashmere throws, good saucepans, and other 'investment' life-nourishing luxuries

✳ getting two or three rooms in shape to reflect your style and make you feel at home until you have the funds to do up the rest

✳ paring down and making a decisive style statement: get rid of anything that clashes with your aesthetic – sell it or take it to a charity shop

✳ updating everything from a junk table with a lick of paint to an sagging armchair with a fresh new flowery loose cover

✳ living with less but carefully selecting the objects you derive most pleasure from

Flower power

Flowers give a space immediate life, colour and scent. I mostly put all of one type in a vase or tank, but mixed bunches of garden roses, lime green alchemilla summer buds and herbs look very pretty and informal. And I also like to mix big blowsy blooms such as roses and peonies in a simple metal buckets on the table for an outdoor summer feast. Here are some notes on my favourite flowers:

Spring   wallflowers, feathery parrot tulips, daffodils, white narcissi, pussy willow, sticky bud branches

Summer   alliums, cut herbs, garden roses (Constance Spry, Gertrude Jekyll, John Clare), rosemary, lavender, peonies, agapanthus, nasturtiums, cornflowers, sunflowers

Autumn   zinnias, ornamental cabbages, anemones, hydrangeas

Winter   forced bulbs for colour and scent in baskets and pots with moss for bedding: narcissi, hyacinths, amaryllis, greenery from the garden to weave into a simple Christmas wreath for the door

making your home human

DON'T AIM FOR PERFECTION. WITH THE EMPHASIS SOLELY ON LOOKS, MANY INTERIOR STYLE BIBLES MISS THE NOTION THAT HOME SHOULD BE AN OASIS OF COMFORT.

Don't be too precious

Be easy on yourself – your home should be relaxed and welcoming, not uptight and squeaky clean. It may be hip to have a sleek East-meets-West white and taupe linen look, but what a bore if you spill the take-out curry or your children make their rabbit a nest on the dry-clean only sofa. Although it would be delicious to slip between freshly laundered linen sheets every day, it actually doesn't matter if you don't have the energy to run an iron over the bedclothes, polish the table until it shines or make the bed with surgical precision.

Buy tough washable fabrics, like canvas and cotton ticking, that can be thrown in the washing machine. I have white cotton loose covers that are a magnet for muddy paw prints but one hot wash cycle swiftly deals with them and they come out as good as new. Likewise, choose wall paints that are easy to wipe down. And if you try to live with less, it's easier to keep your home looking reasonably clean and tidy.

Let in light and keep in warmth

Let daylight flood your home to give it a fresh airy feel; cleaning the windows is one job that is worth doing regularly.

Pools of soft light, whether from lamps or lighted candles, are soothing at night time and can make everyday eating a sensual experience. Never use harsh overhead naked bulbs.

In winter keep your nest warm and cosy with proper insulation, toasty radiators or under-floor heating and, most comforting of all, a roaring wood fire.

Go for what feels good

Natural textures look and feel more comfortable than most synthetics. Opt for soft wool blankets, thick fluffy cotton towels and crisp cotton sheets. Try to avoid the shine factor: satin sheets are too tarty. Likewise, nylon sheets are too trailer park and they give you electric shocks.

Similarly surfaces that are easy to maintain and robust are more pleasing to be with, such as wooden worktops, waxed wood floors, smooth stainless steel kitchen accessories and flat, matt painted finishes.

Upholstery should be robust while yielding just enough so you can sink back and relax amongst soft voluptuous cushions.

Smell sweet

Smell affects our evaluation of things so much so that if you give someone two cans of identical furniture polish, one of which has a pleasant aroma, they will swear that the scented one works better. Thus manufacturers are obsessed with chemically scenting their wares – and boy, do they smell noxious – from the soap powders that claims to make our smalls smell 'tropical' to 'fresh from the fields' air fresheners. Throw them out – be eco and take them to the tip – and fill your home with the natural sensory pleasures of nostalgic cake baking, hot toast and a freshly bees-waxed floor or good scented candle with real floral essences: all honest smells that make our homes desirable places to be.

building your nest

ELASTIC THINKING WILL EASE THE PROCESS OF PLANNING AND REALISING YOUR DREAMS FOR A SNUG AND PRACTICAL HOME.

Find somewhere to roost

If an area is fashionable, house prices will be inflated so it makes some sense to go to the most uncool spot you can find. Many people chant the mantra 'location, location, location', but for me, having swapped a hip-and-happening city pad for a large suburban house with dozens of rooms and a great garden, there is more to life than living where it's supposedly all at.

Once you have decided on the area you wish to target, drive around and view as many properties as possible to get an idea of what you want and what your money will buy. Even if a house or flat isn't obviously for sale or rent, put a note through the letterbox stating your intentions. This is a very good way of avoiding estate agents and their charges.

Be flexible

You may have set your heart on a rose-covered cottage, but if it needs massive restoration it might be more expedient to consider something different, like a decent sixties property that will probably be bigger, in better condition and more light filled. With the money saved, you could also have a little shed in the woods for that romantic getaway. Look for a home with sound bones. Beware of flimsy structures where soundproofing might be negligible, insulation lacking and the finishing third rate.

When you find a property that you like, return several times to view it at different times of the day in order to see how the light changes, if a quiet road assumes motorway proportions at rush hour or whether the next-door neighbours are all-night party groovers.

Be prepared

The uncertainties of house prices and the high cost of moving may lead you to stay put and improve your existing environment. I suggest that you tackle major jobs like the kitchen, bathroom and central heating to enjoy now and that also add value later. The idea of a pricey conservatory might be wonderful, but it's unlikely that you'll recoup the cost when you sell up.

Hired help

Tackle simple jobs yourself, like painting, shelving, and flatpack assembly. Equipment suppliers give out extensive leaflets on how to tackle most jobs, so decide what you might attempt yourself and what is best left to experts, such as plumbing, electrics, gas repairs or removing hazardous materials like asbestos.

Hiring labourers for building and decorating work is where you can loose control and cash, unless you are specific in communicating your needs. This means writing everything down to ensure there are no grey areas, and keeping a close eye on what's being done.

The best way to find a builder is by word of mouth: go and see any previous work that he and his team have done and ask the client whether they finished on time and within budget. Get several estimates before you agreed a price and pay in stages, never upfront. Get the builder to agree to a schedule in writing, but be prepared for those eventualities which are out of everyone's hands, such as bad weather, unexpected rot or delays with materials. Allow a further 10 percent on top of your budget as a safety net.

If you appear to be on the case (don't go on holiday the day they start) are polite (it's tough putting up with strangers making a mess in your home, but they are doing a job) you are more likely to get the job done to your satisfaction and on time. Builders' pet hates are histrionics and changes of mind.

Golden rules

* Plan ahead any outside jobs, such as roofing, pointing and exterior painting, that are best done during the summer months. The optimum time for any garden work is during spring when the ground is neither too dry nor too frozen.

* Wear old clothes, or invest in a pair of painters' overalls.

* When painting and sanding, cover floors and furniture with dust sheets.

* When painting, mask off any areas that you want to avoid with low-tack tape.

* If the kitchen is out of action, rig up a temporary one with a camping stove and microwave. Try to ensure that you have some access to water.

* Stock up on tea and coffee for the builders. It helps to make them feel loved, so they will be more likely to do a better finished job.

* Don't let the builders get at your vacuum cleaner - plaster dust and sawdust spell death to the domestic hoover. Hire an industrial one.

* Look up the address of your local tip and skip hire company as dustmen will not take away half-finished paint cans or building rubble. Skips need licences, so apply to your local council.

creating a mood board

GIVE IDEAS FOCUS WITH A MOOD BOARD, USING SAMPLES OF COLOURS AND FABRICS. BUY A THICK PIECE OF WHITE CARD – NO MORE THAN A METRE SQUARE – AND SECURE SWATCHES TO IT WITH PINS, MASKING TAPE OR SPRAY-MOUNT GLUE.

Fabrics

Use vibrant fabrics as accent colours against a canvas of white, lavender or grey. I have a passion for fuchsia pink cotton velvet, pink muslin and lime green checks, which I make into simple cushions and blinds.

1. Creamy calico A utilitarian fabric available in various weights. Use the heaviest for chair covers and cushions. Buy from haberdashery departments or wholesalers for larger quantities. Pre-shrink before use.

2. Gingham cotton Basic, but sweet. Looks good as chair covers, cushions, simple curtains and decorated lamps. Gingham looks really groovy when used in a domestic goddess pinny (see pages 130–31).

3. Tana lawn cotton I can't think of anything better than Liberty floral prints, which come in such beautiful colours and patterns. Not cheap, but tana lawn cotton is very tough and can be made up into cushions and floaty curtains.

4. Polka-dot cotton Retro spots are everywhere and, like checks or stripes, have a classic utilitarian appeal. Use for pretty cushions (see pages 140–41), aprons, linings for laundry bags and for summer ideas like an itsy bitsy polka-dot bikini.

5. Striped cotton ticking I choose bold blue-and-white stripes for outdoors – deckchairs, awnings, windbreaks and so on – and more subtle woven ticking which looks simple yet contemporary made up into curtains (see pages 146–7) and chair covers.

Trims and ties, ribbons and bows I collect lengths of ribbon and rick-rack to use as edgings on cushions, lampshades, sheets and to make pretty ties for pillowcases, bags and other accessories.

Wallpaper

Bold geometric and floral prints make a more decisive statement than less exuberant patterns and work well along just one wall, a good budget option. One of my favourite looks is a country garden flower print (see pages 44–5 and 68–9).

Paint

Flat matt emulsion and eggshell finishes look more natural and have an appealing opaque effect. Around the house brilliant white emulsion is really adaptable – wraparound white can update a tired interior for not much financial outlay.

For rooms with calm and natural background colour I like to use mint greens, pale lavenders, and soft country creams which allow me to punctuate with splashes of bright colour in cushions, flowers and other details.

For the most part, subtropical zones and hot climates excepting, hot pinks, blues, oranges and other strong colours need to be used with caution to avoid colour overkill. Having said this, it's great to liven up a piece of furniture with cornflower blue painted detail (see pages 136–7) or to make a workspace sing with great pink and white painted stripes (see pages 118–19). The secret is to use clear, bright colours and to avoid anything that has the harshness of day-glo shades that mass manufacturers uses to colour everything from cars to cooking pots.

hot pink

lavender

gingham checks and polka dots

floral tana
lawn cotton

country florals

strawberry pink

pale blue

sludgy blue

cornflower

bean green

soft green

mint green

chalk white

blue and
white stripes

ribbons and
rickrack

planning and sketching

PUT YOUR DECORATING IDEAS DOWN ON PAPER. DRAW A BASIC ROOM PLAN TO GET AN IDEA OF WHERE EVERYTHING MIGHT GO AND A SIMPLE SKETCH TO GET A FEEL FOR THE COLOURS AND FABRICS YOU WANT TO USE.

A plan drawn onto squared paper allows you to accurately map out where all the services, such as electrical points and plumbing, will be and whether everything fits into the space. Don't fuss too much about your drawing skills – I suggest working in pencil if you're unsure – mistakes can be rubbed out – and colouring in with watercolour or coloured pencil. If necessary, the final versions can be finished with thin pen lines for extra definition.

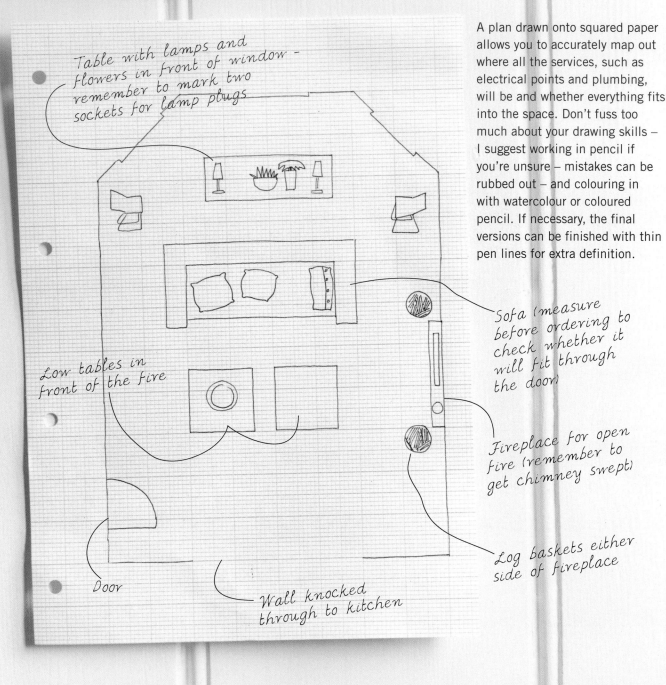

Table with lamps and flowers in front of window – remember to mark two sockets for lamp plugs

Low tables in front of the fire

Door

Wall knocked through to kitchen

Sofa (measure before ordering to check whether it will fit through the door)

Fireplace for open fire (remember to get chimney swept)

Log baskets either side of fireplace

Plan
Title: Sitting Room   Scale 1:20

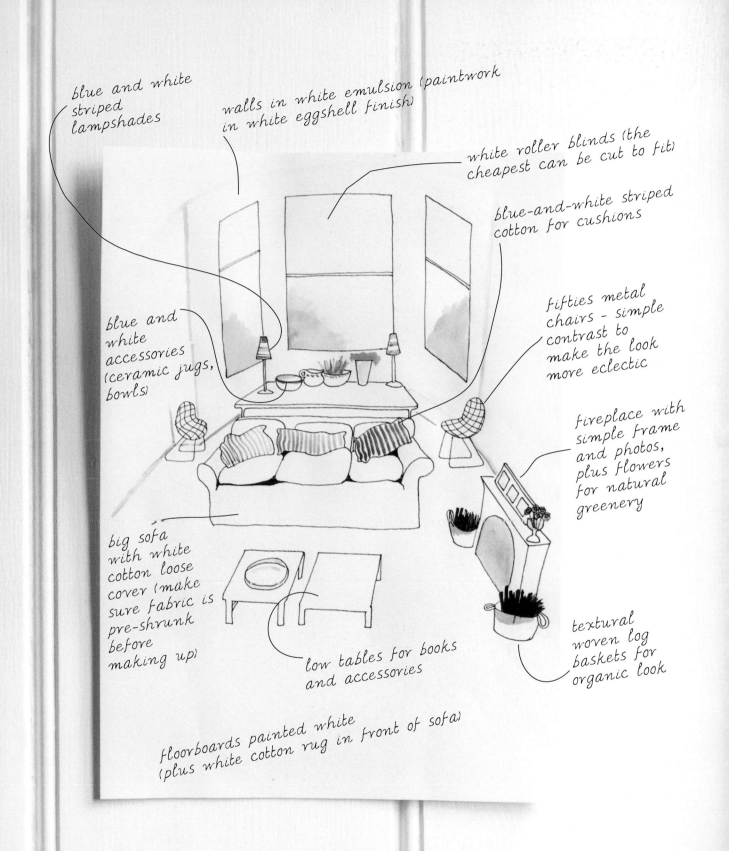

blue and white striped lampshades

walls in white emulsion (paintwork in white eggshell finish)

white roller blinds (the cheapest can be cut to fit)

blue-and-white striped cotton for cushions

blue and white accessories (ceramic jugs, bowls)

fifties metal chairs – simple contrast to make the look more eclectic

fireplace with simple frame and photos, plus flowers for natural greenery

big sofa with white cotton loose cover (make sure fabric is pre-shrunk before making up)

low tables for books and accessories

textural woven log baskets for organic look

floorboards painted white (plus white cotton rug in front of sofa)

Sketch
A simple plan: blue and white sitting room – fresh, modern and airy

top 10 decorating tools

HAVING A BASIC TOOL KIT IS THE ONLY WAY TO PRACTICE HOME DIY, WITHOUT IT NO JOB CAN BE COMPLETED EFFICIENTLY. I KNOW THAT EVERY SELF-RESPECTING BUILDER OR DIY AFICIONADO WILL OWN A FAR GRANDER AND MORE EXTENSIVE BATTERY OF USEFUL GADGETS, BUT HERE ARE TEN ITEMS THAT I MUST HAVE TO HAND BEFORE I TACKLE THE MOST FREQUENTLY EXECUTED DECORATING JOBS.

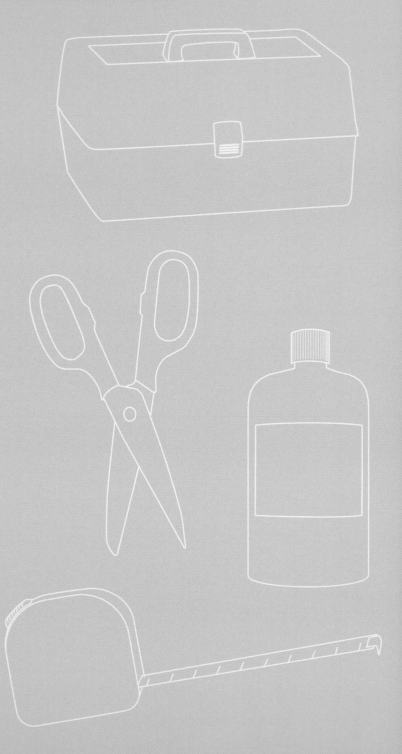

1 **tool box**
You need somewhere to put all your tools, otherwise a state of disorganisation occurs. I use a simple plastic box with a click lid that opens up to reveal a removable top shelf, with compartments for storing nails, screws and wallplugs, and space below for bigger items, like claw hammers and screwdrivers.

2 **sharp scissors**
For cutting everything from wallpaper to string.

3 **extending tape measure**
25m is best for most measuring jobs.

4 **white spirit**
Absolutely essential for cleaning oil-based paints off brushes (water is fine for emulsion).

5 **paintbrushes**
A set of four will tackle nearly all jobs: 100mm brush for emulsion, 50mm and 25mm for oil-based paint and 12mm cutting-in brush for window frames and straight lines.

6 **paint roller**
Quicker than a brush for applying emulsion to walls and ceilings. Sponge rollers are cheaper, but spatter paint. Lambswool and mohair best.

7 **spirit level**
For keeping all straight lines straight.

8 **sandpaper**
In different grades. Also a block of wood to wrap paper around for smoothing or keying surfaces.

9 **pencil**
HB is best for marking measurements on walls and other surfaces.

10 **filler**
Makes even the most ravaged and pitted walls presentable. Use all-purpose for wood and plaster.

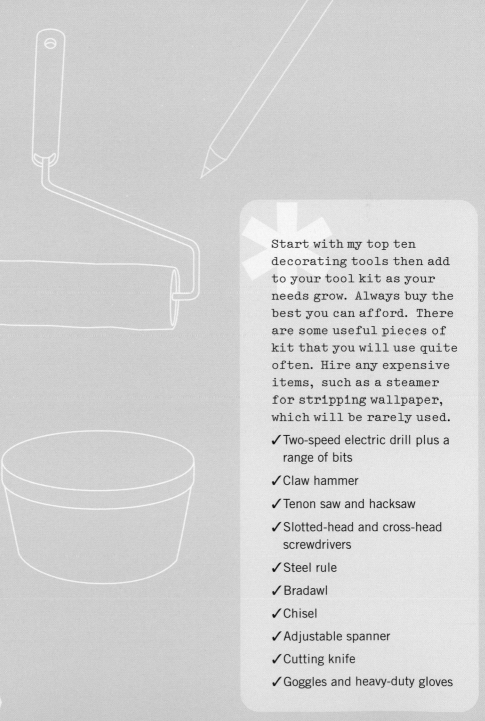

Start with my top ten decorating tools then add to your tool kit as your needs grow. Always buy the best you can afford. There are some useful pieces of kit that you will use quite often. Hire any expensive items, such as a steamer for stripping wallpaper, which will be rarely used.

✓ Two-speed electric drill plus a range of bits

✓ Claw hammer

✓ Tenon saw and hacksaw

✓ Slotted-head and cross-head screwdrivers

✓ Steel rule

✓ Bradawl

✓ Chisel

✓ Adjustable spanner

✓ Cutting knife

✓ Goggles and heavy-duty gloves

decorating clinic

HERE ARE MY ANSWERS TO SOME COMMON DECORATING DILEMMAS.

Q: What will the neighbours think? I don't like curtains and want as much light as possible to flood in through my windows, but can I leave them bare?

A: Even if nosy neighbours are not your concern, you must surely agree that a degree of modesty is required in the bathroom or lavatory. A simple roller blind in white cotton or even a panel of stretched muslin will provide a screen but at the same time filter the light. Alternatively, consider fitting opaque glass.

Q: Can I decorate with pink or is it strictly for sissies?

A: I thoroughly recommend it. Although shocking Schiaparelli fuchsia is my favourite pink for lipstick, I would stop short at washing my walls all over in such a loud shade. Why not paint a wall in strawberry pink ice-cream coloured stripes – a groovy choice, even for a macho teenager (see pages 118–19).

Q: My bedroom is teeny weeny. How can I make it look bigger?

A: You can't go wrong with wraparound white to create an illusion of space. I also suggest that you think about building simple cupboards and using your bed for under storage. Be ruthless in removing any clutter and only have what you need and use regularly.

Q: How cool is it to colour co-ordinate?

A: Like dressing from head-to-toe in black, as urban creative types are prone to, plunging a room into monotone is frankly very dull. Unless you want an impersonal hotel-foyer look, I suggest you play with colour and have fun with it. (I am particularly fond of plain white backgrounds against which I put shots of bright colour – pink or mint green, for example – in furniture and objects.

Q: How do I please a demanding teenage daughter?

A: Make her feel like a princess with one of those floaty mosquito net devices (see pages 72–3) and some great coloured bed linen. Let her flood the room with pink light even if it makes the room look like a brothel, burn evil-smelling joss sticks, play loud rock music (between 8pm and 9pm only) and cover her walls with as many teeny boy band pin-ups as she desires. At least there will a few less issues to argue about.

Q: I've spent months trying to find the perfect white. I'm down to a shortlist of fifty, so what do I do next?

A: Life's too short to fret over such details unless you're rich enough to employ someone to do the choosing for you. Remember that a paint sample takes on a different colour when it's transposed to a whole room, and can therefore lead you into more agonising. I suggest you go straight to your favourite builders' merchant and ask for his best brilliant white matt emulsion. Trust me, it will look fab!

Q: Art. Yes or no?

A: If there's nothing that you desire to see every minute of the day, then leave your walls bare. There's no need to have pictures on the wall just because you feel you ought to and the Have-Everythings down the road do. I am very keen on black-and-white family photos (see pages 138–9).

Q: I can't afford to box in my radiators. How can I make them less obtrusive?

A: Live with them, but help them melt into the background by painting the same colour as the walls. There are now some very good radiator paints on the market.

Q: It's going to cost squillions to carpet my stairs. Any tips?

A: Have you thought about painting them instead? It is much cheaper and really stylish, but you will have to educate the family in negotiating them using fairy-like steps (see pages 28–9).

Q: What about beige?

A: Too safe and too dull. Avoid it at all costs. I once interviewed the late society decorator David Hicks who said it was the colour his clients demanded most, so it only goes to show that cash doesn't equal decorating sense. Beige-like colours should only be allowed if they are naturally so, such as a soft wool blanket and woven baskets.

Q: I'm moving out of the city but don't want to abandon all my urban sensibilities. Can I do country without the chintz?

A: Absolutely, so long as you stay clear of kitchen airers festooned with dried flowers, herbs and shelves groaning with blue and white china. Agas are allowed.

Q: What's the cheapest way to store kitchen plates and other crockery?

A: Keep control of your mind and life with simple open shelves for all your kitchen goods. DIY stores usually have lengths of wood and simple brackets. Alternatively you could recycle old shelving that you might have from somewhere else in the house.

Q: What can I do with the perfectly hideous dining suite that my mother-in-law donated to us. My husband won't part with it.

A: He probably doesn't like it anyway but feels duty bound to keep it. Proceed with cunning and advertise it on eBay. If you get a good offer, dangle it in front of him: the lure of some 'holding and folding' might just do the trick!

make and do

WITH THE SENSE OF COMFORT IT PROVIDES, DOMESTICITY IS EVER MORE APPEALING, IN OUR QUICK-FIX SOCIETY. MAKING SIMPLE THINGS FOR ONESELF GIVES THAT WARM FEELING OF WELLBEING AND ACHIEVEMENT.

Just as baking a birthday cake and decorating it with baubles and candles is so much more pleasurable than coming home with a perfectly formed, but not-half-as-tasty specimen from the store, so running up a pretty cushion or trimming a blanket is more satisfying, and individual, than what is available to buy in the shops.

You don't have to use up all your precious spare time slaving over a sewing machine. Specifically making the time to do a simple project is good for the soul and allows you to concentrate on something a little more creative than the latest soap opera. All the ideas in this book have simple instructions and are easy to follow and execute.

They will also help you to save money as this book is about being resourceful and making the most of what you've got. For example, don't get rid of the paint dregs from a decorating job as there might be enough left over to renovate a junk table (see pages 124–5). Likewise, don't throw away old clothes: if they are in a great print, cut them up and use fabric for appliqué or re-invent it as a cushion or simple bag. Similarly hunt around charity shops, where you will certainly find some treasures like a perfectly good cream blanket that can be jazzed up with a velvet trim, or a tablecloth that can be dyed for a new look.

sewing essentials

* Sewing machine – buy a basic model if you're a beginner
* Fabric remnants – save any pieces left over from sewing jobs and collect scraps from sales
* Trimmings – save any ribbons, rickrack and bows from gifts
* Work box – store everything in a plastic crate or set aside a shelf or two in your workspace. Use a separate bag for your remnants and trimmings
* Dressmaker's tape measure
* Ruler – for drawing straight lines
* Tailors' chalk – for marking fabric, use white for dark fabrics and coloured for patterns
* All-purpose scissors – for cutting out paper patterns
* Large dressmaking scissors – for cutting fabric
* Small embroidery scissors – for cutting threads
* Assorted sewing needles – for tacking, stitching and hemming
* Tacking thread – easy to break when unpicking tacking stitches
* Unpicker – a hooked device to help remove stitches and tacking stitches
* Steam iron and ironing board
* Fabric dye – machine washable ones are best and can be used to dye both cottons and synthetics
* Elastic
* Touch-and-close tape – useful for closing cushions
* Buttons – a tin of spare buttons is always useful
* Safety pins

key sewing tips

The secret to good sewing is a straight seam. Practise on small scraps of material to get going. Pinning and tacking are key when stitching two or three pieces of fabric together so they don't slip out of position when running through the machine. To make a seam, pin and tack the right sides of the fabric together. Remove the pins and machine stitch. Remove the tacking and press the seam open.
There are various ways of neatening seams: fraying fabrics may be fixed by zigzag stitch, either before or after joining the seams, whilst non-fraying fabrics may be turned under and stitched.
To hem a piece of fabric, turn the hem to the wrong side to the required depth, stitch and press; turn the hem over again, pin or tack. Stitch close to the first fold. Press.
It's important to iron as you go along to keep your sewing in shape and easy to handle. Use a stem iron or a damp cloth on the wrong side in order to avoid a shine on the fabric. Don't forget that seams must be dampened before ironing so they lie flat.

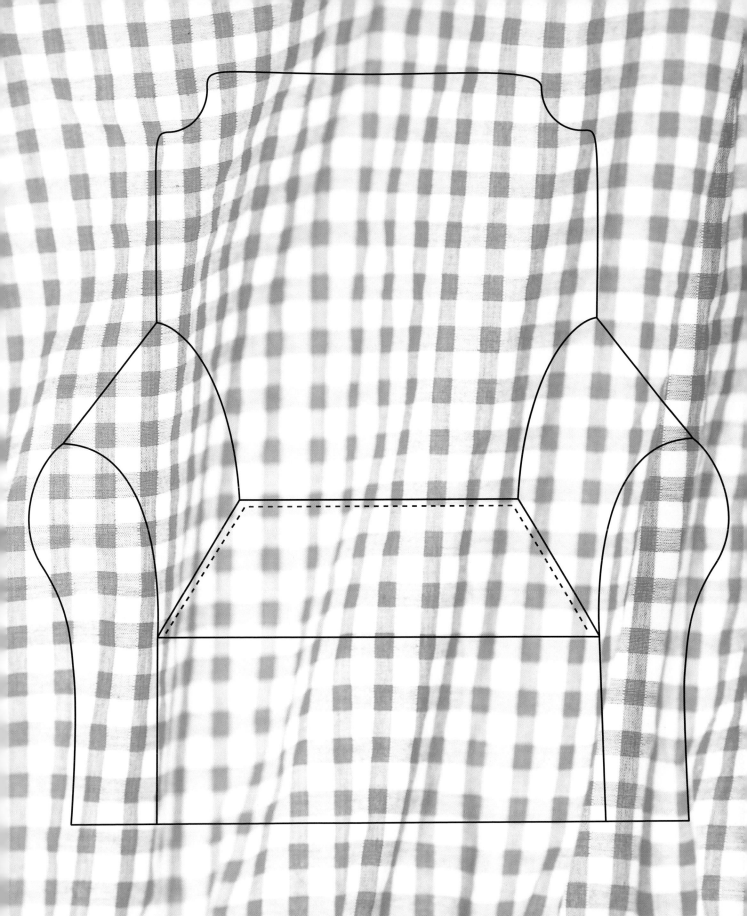

PART 2

Decorating secrets

step inside

10 WAYS TO MAKE A STYLISH ENTRANCE

1 Paint the front door in a fresh light colour - my favourite is seaside or duck-egg blue - in tough exterior eggshell. No gloss paint, please.

2 Ensure that the front door is in keeping with the architectural style and period of the building.

3 Open up a dark hallway with layers of fresh white paint. If you prefer colour, go for muted shades of blue, green and lavender in small spaces. Larger spaces will not be overwhelmed by brighter shades, like tulip pink or emerald green.

4 For a dramatic entrance, invest in a patterned wallpaper - a fabulous floral, geometric or bold stripe, for example, looks good in cramped spaces. Wallpaper is not as economical as paint, but you can see exactly what you're getting.

5 Lay down the thickest, scratchiest doormat you can find to deal with muddy feet. Alternatively, fit some heavy-duty jute matting like carpet, either as a doormat-sized piece by the door or a length stretching down the hallway.

6 Think ergonomically. Position the hall light switch immediately to the right of the front door so there's no fumbling in the dark. Install coat hooks to the left, preferably above a radiator to help dry wet coats.

7 Fill the biggest vase you have with some seasonal blooms - pussy willow in spring, a dewy bunch of summer garden roses or a few autumnal allotment-grown dahlias.

8 Be completely ruthless, or at least try, and banish as much family clutter as you can. Install big baskets to store any clobber that gets dropped.

9 Hang a large mirror in the hallway to increase the sense of space and to check that you're looking pulled-together before flying out of the house.

10 Make sure the lighting is welcoming, try a pretty chandelier, a simple pendant shade or a lamp on a side table. Recessed spotlights are also an option but I think they look more hotel-like than home-sweet-home.

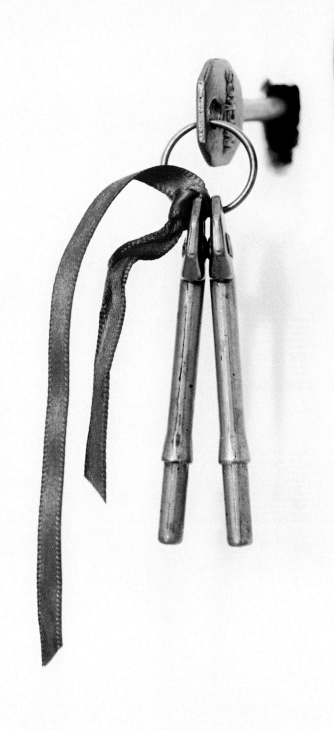

stairway to heaven

CREATE A SENSE OF AIRY LIGHTNESS WITH A STAIRWAY PAINTED IN A FRESH WHITE COLOUR SCHEME, WHICH IS HARDY ENOUGH TO WITHSTAND BUSY FAMILY TRAFFIC.

Providing noise is not an issue, there is absolutely nothing undressed about bare stairs, despite what your mother might say. When it comes to style, be firm, hold out for what you want and, most importantly, don't threaten that not-inconsequential matter of the budget. Going back to – or rather up and down – the stair question, I think there is nothing simpler or more stylish than sanded and painted stairs, either fully painted or with a central strip left unpainted to look like a runner. Paint is much cheaper than wool or sisal runners, which are not only costly but also need to be cut and fitted to size, a further expense as you'll need a professional to do it.

To achieve this look, pull on a pair of rubber gloves and thoroughly clean the stair treads with a bucket of hot water, detergent and a good scrubbing brush. When the stairs are completely dry, measure the width of the runner in from both edges and mark with two parallel strips of masking tape. Using a small paintbrush, apply a wood primer and undercoat then finish off with two top coats of white floor paint. Don't use anything other than floor paint as it will not be tough enough. If your stairs are already painted, you could mask off the 'runner' area and paint it in a contrasting colour – say white with a blue or a Shaker-style brick red strip.

A bare wood runner is most practical for cleaning: either brush or vacuum off any dust and mop with a damp cloth and detergent. Don't wax or polish the runner part as this will make it precariously slippery.

If the banisters and spindles of your staircase are in good condition, upkeep with a wax polish. If not, don't worry that you're being cruel to a good piece of mahogany, cover it up with a lick of eggshell paint.

ingredients

* Walls painted in white emulsion
* Woodwork painted in white oil-based eggshell
* Stairs sanded and painted with white floor paint, bar a central strip to look like a runner
* Floors sanded and painted with white floor paint
* Mahogany banister and spindles sanded and waxed
* A posh frock for making a glamorous descent

tip TREAD CAREFULLY If you want to paint your stairs all over and still fit in family life, there is a way! Starting at the top, paint every other stair. Whilst the paint is drying, use the alternate unpainted stairs. When the paint is completely dry, the other steps can be painted.

big ideas

BEAN GREEN WALLS AND OVERSIZED FLOWERHEADS GIVE A RELAXED ORGANIC FLAVOUR TO A NARROW HALLWAY, WHERE SPACE AND LIGHT ARE AT A PREMIUM.

Built to make the maximum use of limited space, small houses are frequently compromised on the area devoted to an entrance hall, with little room to navigate a pushchair let alone swing the proverbial cat. As hallways are often cramped, and frankly incompatible with clutter, they aren't terribly convenient thoroughfares for family homes. As embarking on structural rearrangements is out of the question for most of us, it is financially more agreeable to make the most of what you've got.

Start by maximising the available light sources. A glazed front door and fanlight will make the most of any natural daylight, particularly crucial during short winter days.

Although white does open up a restricted space, consider an organic hue like this bean green on the walls. It is pleasing to the eye and echoes the natural greenery of the front garden – a sort of uninterrupted colour flow from exterior to interior. Shots of pink provided by the blowsy hydrangeas add contrast and accentuate the natural feel.

It makes perfect sense in a long skinny hallway to install a narrow table that will underneath house baskets for footballs, Wellingtons and all the usual outdoor clobber.

There's nothing like going over the top with a giant globe paper lantern – a real sixties retro idea which still looks good. Now, you may think this is the last thing anyone would want in a teeny-weeny hallway, but, like magic, large objects in small spaces can actually increase the perceived sense of space. Try the same trick by putting a huge mirror in a small sitting room or a king-size bed in a box room. By the way, this trickery of the eye does not work in reverse – a minuscule light in a big hall, will look, well, pretty pathetic.

For protection against a brigade of dirty feet, fit a heavy-duty doormat over wooden pine boards that have been sanded and sealed. The floor will deal with an enormous amount of wear and tear and need only the minimum of upkeep with a mop down and occasional re-waxing.

tip

HOW TO PAINT

✳ Dip the brush in the paint to cover half the bristle length. Wipe off any excess paint on the side of the tin.

✳ Lay the paint on by applying a horizontal band approximately 20cm wide and brush out sideways. Finish with light strokes in a criss-cross pattern.

✳ Hold a small paintbrush like a pencil, but hold a large paintbrush like a beach bat.

✳ If using a roller, load it with paint by pushing it back and forth in the front of the tray, then do the same on the slope of the tray to spread the paint evenly over the roller.

✳ Roll slowly and evenly until the area is covered.

✳ Do not load the roller with too much paint and take the roller off the wall carefully to prevent splashing.

✳ ingredients

✳ **Front door with glazed panels and a fanlight to make the most of the limited light**

✳ **Walls painted in bean green emulsion**

✳ **Wooden floorboards sanded and waxed**

✳ **Heavy-duty doormat fixed like fitted carpet**

✳ **Long narrow wooden hall table**

✳ **Large glass vase with the last of the summer hydrangeas**

✳ **Oversized paper globe lantern**

smart and simple

HARDWORKING GINGHAM COTTON AND CERAMIC TILES FOR A STYLISH ENTRANCE.

Treat your hall as you would any other room and make it as pleasingly functional as you can. It is true that you don't linger in an entrance as long as other spaces, but it creates the first impression of your home and needs to beguile guests.

Creating a sense of space and openness in the hallway is key. Here it has been achieved with fresh white paint, a bare tiled floor and a large mirror, also painted white, to reflect the light back from the glazed doorway.

Another idea for a hard-wearing floor, which doesn't necessarily need to be protected by rugs and runners, is lino tiles that can be laid in a simple chequer board pattern. You could also consider tough studded rubber tiles or even cork, which is making something of a comeback.

Seize upon any chance to play and punch in some great colour with soft furnishings. I have dressed a couple of sixties wooden side chairs in pull-on purple gingham cotton covers. The fabric is washable and so will easily cope with the moment when little Johnny drops his ice-cream cornet. As well as covering side chairs, which can be pulled in as reserves around the dining table, you could also cover an uninteresting hall table in a piece of striped ticking or check cloth edged with velvet ribbon for a really smart look.

To reiterate, damage-proof elements are crucial in the hallway. Pram wheels spell death to anything precious or antique, so I would not advise displaying your fanciest pieces. Instead opt for church candles on a hallway table for Christmas or in summer stuff vases with sprigs of rosemary to set the scene for feasting out in the garden. Simple touches like fresh flowers can cheer up even the most impersonal hallway.

ingredients

* Walls painted in white emulsion
* Woodwork painted in white eggshell
* Large mirror painted in white eggshell to reflect the available light
* Industrial-style enamel pendant lampshade
* Sixties beech chairs dressed in gingham cotton covers (see page 122)
* Antique ceramic-tiled floor

period feature

If you are restoring and renovating an old house and are lucky enough to have intact ceramic floor tiles, it's likely that they'll need a really good clean. Detergent and water alone will not be strong enough so go to a builders' merchant to buy a specialist cleaner that will remove ingrained dirt. The floor can then be sealed with a clear and matt varnish that will keep maintenance down to mopping as necessary. Cracked or loose tiles can be fixed using a two-part epoxy resin adhesive. Remove any dust and dirt from the tile spaces before commencing repairs.

cool country

STYLISH TEXTURES THAT ARE TOUGH AND HARD-WEARING.

Rural life is often fantasised about by urbanites who rarely have to grapple with power cuts, uninvited insects or small people watching tv whilst wearing Wellington boots caked in mud (far too mucky for the lifestyle magazines). With this last point in mind, it is prudent to choose a robust floorcovering for the thoroughfares in a country abode. The sealed terracotta floor tiles seen here are perfect for dealing with dirt.

Don't throw up your hands, chapped from all that fresh air and digging, at the thought of laying a lovely white floor runner to skim the length of a well-trafficked hallway or passage. There is a trick: buy the cotton variety. Rag rugs are equally good. When necessary, throw it in the washing machine or soak it in the bath and leave it to dry al fresco. Watch out for strong colours, though, as the dye may run.

The wash-and-wear approach also applies to the wall surfaces. I have known everything from septic tank scrapings, sticky handprints and pig fat to leave their marks on the walls. It is always useful to have a pot of emulsion to hand for dealing with such irritations.

Keep the entrance space free from excess boxes, laundry, piles of books and toys to suggest an orderly visual flow. A simple table – a beaten-up junk buy, painted with a single coat of emulsion and then unevenly rubbed down with sandpaper for an aged effect – and flowers are always appropriate. Placing a chair, table or even a mirror at the end of the space creates a pleasing sense of perspective.

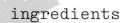

ingredients

* Walls and woodwork painted in white emulsion
* Terracotta tiled floor
* Side table painted in emulsion and rubbed down with sandpaper for a rustic feel
* Washable white cotton floor runner
* Metal lantern for candles
* Flowers in a simple glass jug

tip PAINTING WALLS   Before painting, wash interior walls down using a sponge and apply an undercoat. Finish with two coats of emulsion. Work in 60cm bands with a roller, starting in the top right- hand corner if you are right handed or the top left- hand corner if you are left handed and ending in the opposite bottom corner above the skirting. Use a brush to ' cut in' the narrow strip around the door and window frames after the main section of wall has been painted.

chill

10 WAYS TO MAKE A RELAXING LIVING SPACE

1 Your chill-out space need not be a whole room, especially if your nest is small. A sofa dressed with squashy cushions and squeezed into a snug corner of a kitchen or dining room can work just as well.

2 Chairs look cool dressed in simple pull-on loose covers with maybe a tie here or a button detail there. Use tough machine-washable woven cotton and calico. Natural linen is also good but creases, so it's not for fussers. Pre-shrink all fabrics before use.

3 Buy the biggest sofa you can afford – a good one should have a solid hardwood frame with a sprung base and back. Second-hand buys from the forties or earlier might need bodywork but they're made of sturdy stuff and will be cheaper than a modern equivalent.

4 Feather-filled cushions are soft and yielding, but need plumping daily to maintain their shape. Do not bother with cheap foam cushion pads as they are not worth it for either looks or comfort.

5 I prefer calm, soft pools of light from table lamps with pretty shades trimmed with ribbons. Paper parchment shades are good. Dark walls absorb more light than paler ones so choose the wattage of your bulbs accordingly. Try to use low-energy lightbulbs, which last longer and are more energy efficient than ordinary ones.

6 Build a blazing fire with smokeless fuel or logs. Sweep the chimney if it has not been used for some time. Basic radiators look fine against white walls, but not so good against coloured ones. Consider painting them to match. Or install radiator-free underfloor heating.

7 Sunny south-facing sitting rooms that let in lots of light are tremendously uplifting on winter days. In summer, benefit from doors or windows that open onto the garden or terrace.

8 Blue and white is my number one chill-out colour combo – it looks classic yet modern and never dates. Key elements include soft white, duck-egg blue or eau-de-nil walls teamed with striped cotton ticking and checks.

9 Use natural textures and scents for a living, breathing space. Try roughly woven baskets, fibrous rugs and woolly throws. Burn tea lights in jars or light a good scented candle (such as tuberose by Diptyque) that actually smells of what it claims to.

10 Wall-to-wall carpets don't suit a light and airy look, so stick to mats or rugs for added texture and warmth underfoot. Painted white floorboards are easy to achieve. (See page 90.)

big sofas are best

COMFY SEATING TO SPRAWL ON AND BLUE AND WHITE DETAILS ARE KEY INGREDIENTS FOR A LIGHT AND AIRY SITTING ROOM.

Divide the living room into a series of zones to create a more inviting and layered look. I like to position a slim table behind the sofa, which provides a focal point for the eye and a handy space for lamps – useful for reading by – and flowers. If this space is by a window, even better, as the eye is drawn to a further area of interest outside.

On a technical note, think about installing floor-mounted electrical sockets to power centrally positioned lamps. If you're starting from scratch, it's worth roughly planning the arrangement of your furniture so that you know where the electrics need to be routed. See pages 16–17 for tips on drawing up a simple plan.

Then there is the seating itself. Measure up before buying that great ship of a bargain sofa. It would be too, too dreadful to find that it won't squeeze through the front door let alone negotiate hairpin turns around a narrow staircase. Having said that, it is possible to take out windows and hire a man with a winch to haul a really big sofa up to where you need it. It may be worth the effort and expense for a really well made piece that you intend to live with for years. Accessorise your sofa with several squashy cushions – never arranged in stiff rows – and maybe a throw.

Installing a big sofa or two means that you don't need to clutter up the rest of the room. Stick to essential items only. If your floor is bare, the space in front of the sofa where there might be a low table, or a big square foot stool piled with favourite books is the place to have a rug; choose something pretty in stripes, or sisal, or a gorgeous wool, to give texture and colour.

If there's space, you could have two sofas facing each other, so much the better if there is a fireside beside which you can curl up on a drizzly Sunday afternoon.

ingredients

* Walls painted in white emulsion
* Woodwork painted in white eggshell
* Floorboards sanded and painted in white floor paint
* Sofa covered in washable white cotton loose covers
* Blue-and-white striped cotton cushions
* Blue-and-white striped lampshades
* Sixties wooden coffee table
* Fifties wirework side chairs
* White roller blinds
* Woven wicker log baskets

tip

HOW TO PREPARE FOR PAINTING
* Dress in your oldest painting clothes and wear protective headgear
* Place the paint can onto newspaper or a polythene sheet
* Open the paint can with a screwdriver or a large coin
* Stir the paint with a thick stick
* Mix the paint with a circular up-and-down motion
* Emulsion paint that has not been used for a while may have water on top; pour it away
* An oil-based paint will have a skin that should be cut off; sieve the remaining paint through an old pair of tights
* Thin the paint if very thick; use water for emulsion and white spirit for oil-based paints

cool and modern

CHILL OUT WITH SIMPLE RETRO IDEAS.

Streamlined, modern and functional sixties-style furniture is back in vogue and suits the mood for simple living. It's likely that parents and grandparents will be harbouring some really cool relics from the era and might even be persuaded to part with them – my mother-in-law's Saarinen white tulip table and chairs are good examples. The second-hand furniture trade knows the value of these things well, so consequently you have to look harder for bargains.

Do you remember when walls were lined in orange hessian and the groovy thing to do was make lampbases out of Chianti bottles encased in wooden raffia? I suspect there won't be revival of the latter, but I am all for choosing something rough and textural, such as hessian, in stone colours. I have also been toying with the idea of using cork wallpaper, a thin layer of amalgamated cork

ingredients

* **Walls papered sixties-style geometric-print wallpaper**
* **Floor covered with sea grass matting**
* **Sixties-style sideboard**
* **Sixties-style pendant lampshade**
* **Vintage floorlamp**
* **Red canvas curtains**

bonded to backing paper, which has an organic look and that will add colour and texture to a room but maintain a contemporary look. I can see it looking really good in an eco house tucked away in the woods.

Watch out for new interpretations of the sixties look, too. There are some great wallpapers around – a big, bold geometric pattern is a cheap and easy way to make a stunning visual statement in a room.

Finally, the new wave of wallpapers includes photographic papers where digital images are blown up and used across a whole wall. It's pretty expensive but does allow you to indulge in using your photographs and designs as inspiration.

Lighting is another area that is harking back to the swinging days of Minis and Mary Quant. There are some fabulous pendant lamps and hanging shades in moulded plastic that will add that psychedelic edge to your living space.

tip

WALLPAPER PREP

YOU WILL NEED:
* Fold- up pasting table, which can be bought cheaply from a DIY store
* Pasting brush
* 25cm wide wallpaper hanging brush
* Bucket for paste
* Cloth and sponge for smoothing down and removing excess paste
* Seam roller for smoothing edges
* Long spirit level
* Wallpaper scissors
* Tape measure to work out the lengths of paper

childproof and stylish

WASHABLE STRIPES THAT CAN COPE WITH STICKY FINGERS.

It's not so scary, I promise you, to invest in pretty fabrics and furnishing ideas in rooms that house the dangerous combination of a tv and children. My offspring like nothing more than curling up in front of The Simpsons with plates of something sweet and sticky – the remnants of which are usually smeared and crumbled over the chairs. I stoically whip off the covers and give them a good wash at 40 degrees, then when they're still a bit damp, I stretch them back over the seating to look good as new until the next sticky assault.

The key to a child-friendly interior is to make sure that all the other elements in the room are washable, even the rugs, and that all surfaces are wipedown. Use spongeable paint finishes for both walls and woodwork.

It might sound churlish in our child-centred times, but bedrooms apart, there is no need to infantilise your house with untidy piles of toys and playkit. Modern plastic toys are such an eyesore that they need suitable storage for putting back some visual order at the end of the day. I recommend rigid white plastic boxes that can be stacked away in the corner, or old junk shop cupboards that can be painted and used for toys, games, videos and dvds.

Another option is to limit the amount of stuff your children have – does your little darling really need ten MyScene dolls, plus their plastic surfer boyfriends, sports car and film-star sized wardrobes?

tip

HOW TO PAINT A DOOR
* Wash door thoroughly and wedge open. Use a primer/undercoat and apply two top coats. Rub down the paintwork between each coat. Start in the top left hand corner and paint in bands about 50cm wide. Work fast so that the painted bits are joined whilst the paint is still wet.

ORDER TO PAINT A WINDOW
* 1 top sash * 2 bottom sash
* 3 frame and rebates * 4 interior mouldings of window * 5 top and bottom * 6 left and right
* 7 window frame
NB (for a neat finish apply masking tape to edge of panes before painting) scrape paint off the window with a razor blade

ingredients

* **Walls painted in white emulsion**

* **Sanded and scrubbed wooden floorboards, painted with a dark stain**

* **Junk cupboards painted in white eggshell for storing videos and dvds**

* **Armchairs covered in blue-and-white striped cotton loose covers**

* **Washable cotton rugs**

unfussy florals

GIVE COUNTRY BUDS AND BLOOMS A CONTEMPORARY TWIST.

The clever way to do florals – a.k.a the trad country house look – is not to do them to death. Blooms rioting and rambling across walls and every piece of furniture might be the preferred look of the queens of chintz, but to make it look modern you have to be restrained in execution. Here only one wall has been papered with a blowsy rose patterned paper, which makes it a cheaper option.

Combined with simple decorating details – a gingham-trimmed lampshade, a small second-hand sofa updated

with a pull-on loose cotton cover, green-checked cotton cushion covers and spring bulbs in basic flowerpots – the effect is fresh and contemporary.

Going back to the lampshade, yes, this rather dated interior feature is having a renaissance. Usually associated with grandma's comfortable sitting room, the lampshade is returning in a rather more glamorous guise this time around.

The trick is not to rush to the attic to dig out your old peach ruched silk shade, pale, dull and so 'yesterday'. Choose colour, pattern, trimmings or a big, bold silhouette. Shades come in linen, silk, suede, velvet and parchment – my favourite because it diffuses the light beautifully. Treat a lampshade like a gorgeous hat and decorate with ribbon, braids and bows.

I love the vogue for floorstanding lamps with fabulous shades, they look good in a dull corner and also give pleasing height. After years of concealed designer lighting, it's definitely time to put bold decorative lamps back on the agenda.

tip

HOW TO HANG WALLPAPER

✳ Start papering at one side of the largest window in the room and work towards the door.
✳ If using a large pattern paper, hang the first length over the fireplace or the focal point of the room and work away from it in both directions so that the design is central and symmetrical.
✳ It is vital the first piece of paper you hang is straight as it will be the guide for all the rest. Use a spirit level to make a vertical and mark it with pencil or chalk.
✳ Place the strip of wallpaper on the pasting table, apply the paste and leave to soak.
✳ Fold the wallpaper into pleats.
✳ Position the paper along the edge of the vertical line.
✳ Butt the joins and use a wallpaper brush to smooth into position, working from the centre to the edges of paper to remove any bubbles.
✳ Crease the overlaps at the top and bottom of the wall, cut neatly with scissors and brush back into place.
✳ Avoid squeezing paste out of joints.
✳ Wipe off excess paste whilst it is moist using a clean damp sponge.

ingredients

✳ Walls papered in rose-print wallpaper
✳ Floor covered with sisal matting and a wool rug
✳ Sixties wooden side table
✳ Wooden two-seater sofa covered in a white cotton calico cover
✳ Junk lampstand painted in white eggshell with a fabric shade trimmed with gingham (see page 151)

soft light by the fireside

THE ONLY WAY TO SURVIVE DEEP MID-WINTER IS BY TURNING YOUR NEST INTO A COSY RETREAT, WITH SIMPLE INDULGENCES LIKE TEA AND TOAST IN FRONT OF A LOG FIRE.

Deep, rich terracottas and muddy greens are traditional snug, curling-up-in-a-ball colours that work well in the shadows, but walls painted white are modern and light enhancing for wintry rooms.

The bigger the fireplace, the larger the blaze, which is why the small grates found in many old houses are worth enlarging to make simple, modern rectangular openings. A built-in mantelshelf is wide enough but not too wide for candles, art, mirrors and, for those who like to appear busy, important invitations.

The choice of log baskets is crucial – the bigger and more roughly woven the better. I put them beside the fireplace for a rural feel. Never buy those finished with wood stain – they might be really cheap but they look shiny and unnatural. The safety police will note that firesides like this should never be left unattended.

With the warmth factor high on the list of priorities, install underfloor heating pipes beneath terracotta tiled floors to keep the chill off. Underfloor heating is a good solution for anyone who has an aversion to radiators and is laying a completely new floor.

Pools of soft lamp- and candlelight are the best ways to make a winter room both look and feel snug. Slender lamp bases with simple card shades are classic and survive any changes in lighting trends. Less punishing on the eyes are 40 watt bulbs. The eco-conscious will know that low-energy bulbs last between five and ten times longer and use 75 percent less electricity than ordinary tungsten ones.

Just as my lightweight linen separates are returned to the back of wardrobe at the end of summer, my white loose sofa covers are packed away to make way for soft pink heavy cotton ones that suit the wintry mood. For the cushions, cotton in pink checks and a floral sprig print give a modern take on the country look.

ingredients

* Walls in white emulsion
* Terracotta tiled floor
* Large, open fireplace
* Logs in woven baskets
* Blue and white striped cotton rug
* Pink checked and floral print cotton cushions
* Slender lamp base and simple card lampshade
* Tea and toast

tile file

Terracotta tiles are fantastically hard-wearing and, when bought from a local source, are much cheaper than if they are transported from afar. Terracotta is super absorbent so any spills will be permanently visible unless you seal the tiles as soon as they're laid. I have found that applying two coats of linseed oil provides protection against red wine, grease and the usual domestic stains. Before applying the oil, clean the unsealed tiles with a damp cloth to remove any surface dust. Using a brush, apply the oil to the tiles in a thin layer. Allow to dry for approximately 12 hours before applying a second coat – two coats should suffice. Thereafter, daily maintenance is minimal – sweep and mop down with a mild detergent.

make the difference

colour

Nothing is harder than getting colour right in the home. Most of us have little colour sense so the best thing is to go to your local DIY or paint shop and grab those paint cards with edited ranges rather than the chunky ones with a daunting choice of hundreds of colours. Buy a sample pot of your chosen colour, paint a 50cm square patch and then watch to see how it changes during natural daylight and then at night in artificial light.

Colour alters depending on the light that falls on it. Daylight tends to be bluer than artificial light, which is more constant as it isn't moving like the sun.

"change your look with just a lick of paint"

North facing rooms are darker and need warm colours like soft yellows; south facing rooms can have harsh shadows and glare so cooler blues and greens will work well (wrap around white can be overpowering so it is best to use with splashes of contrasting colour).

Rooms facing east are warmer in the morning with more yellow light from the sunrise which cools as the day progresses; west facing rooms are best at sunset and feel colder in the morning; walls that have direct light appear lighter and walls that surround a window fall into shadow so colours will appear darker.

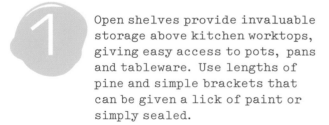

eat

10 WAYS TO MAKE A PRACTICAL KITCHEN

1 Open shelves provide invaluable storage above kitchen worktops, giving easy access to pots, pans and tableware. Use lengths of pine and simple brackets that can be given a lick of paint or simply sealed.

2 My children are messy cooks, and so am I, which is why the floor needs to be as robust and stain resistant as possible. Waxed floorboards, sealed terracotta tiles and good old-fashioned linoleum are all surfaces that can withstand a battering.

3 If you inherit a fitted kitchen you hate, don't rip it out. Revamp it. Simply replace the doors; basic tongue-and-groove makes a far cheaper option than starting all over again.

4 Less is more. Resist the temptation to accumulate kitchen clutter. Most cooking tasks can be executed with the minimum – Le Creuset pans, several wooden spoons, a large stainless steel pasta pot, sharp knives and a basic food processor.

5 Work surfaces that work. Beech and maple are excellent. Beware wet pans, which leave black rings. Marble is fabulous as it doesn't encourage bug growth, but it hates lemon juice and other acids which produce opaque stains. Stainless steel is lovely but perfectionists may angst over scratches that are all part of ordinary wear and tear.

6 Good task lighting. Resist the urge to pepper the ceiling with downlighters. Restrict spots and pendant lights to the area directly above the work surface. Strip lighting under an eye level shelf is also worth considering for chopping and mixing tasks.

7 A decent-sized table. Buy the biggest your space allows. Some swear by round ones – good for bay windows – but I prefer rectangular shapes. My sturdy table is used by all the family for homework and writing, and has often squeezed in twelve for loud Sunday lunches.

8 Windows – to let natural light and air in, as well as kitchen fug out – are key for the room at the heart of the home. I chose to put my kitchen in what was a sitting room, rather than settle for the original but dark and gloomy kitchen space.

9 Everyone should have an old-fashioned larder, keeping cheese at the correct room temperature and yesterday's apple crumble cool. The next best thing is a tall larder fridge for storing perishables at above-freezing temperatures.

10 Simple table accessories. White cotton or linen tablecloths and napkins, cream candles and a vase with a rose or two from the garden are all you need for a simple feast. Plus, of course, some wholesome, fresh foodie ingredients.

budget modern

HOW TO MAKE A KITCHEN PRACTICAL, SIMPLE AND STYLISH USING FLATPACK MDF.

Status-symbol kitchens can cost the earth. The antidote to this conspicuous consumption in culinary matters is MDF. This humble material is practical and stylish, despite being cheap. Made from wood fibres mixed with a non-toxic resin, MDF is similar to chipboard, it can be cleanly cut, nailed or screwed and its surface can be either stained or painted. Basic flatpack MDF kitchen carcasses – cupboards, drawers and shelves – are sold ready to go in just about every builders' merchants so you don't have to place an order months in advance. Measurements are usually a standard 600mm (2ft) deep and 500mm (1ft 8in) wide for a single unit. A basic framework like this can also provide the core for fitting doors in wood or other laminates. When measuring up allow for any pipe work that might need to be incorporated in the cupboard space, such as under sink plumbing.

When space is tight, a single run of basic units comprising sink, worktop and cooker is most useful, especially in rooms of narrow proportions. Together with a

ingredients

* **Basic MDF kitchen carcasses, including units and drawers**
* **Basic stainless-steel sink and taps**
* **Hanging rail made from a metal pole cut to size**
* **Reclaimed wood shelving painted in white eggshell**
* **Splashback made from basic white rectangular ceramic tiles**
* **Walls painted in white vinyl silk emulsion**
* **Wooden blockboard worksurface**
* **Industrial-style glass pendant lights**

tip

FLATPACK PANIC

* Allow plenty of time, don't even think about rushing it.
* Allow plenty of space, and make sure the finished item will fit into room it's destined for.
* Ensure you have all the correct tools before you start.
* Unpack everything carefully and tick off all the parts, checking for any damage.
* Lay out and identify all the pieces before assembly.
* Don't force any joints or screws if they aren't fitting.
* Wait until the end to tighten all the screws in case of problems that mean undoing all your work.

large catering-style oven, this simple arrangement will cover most families' basic kitchen needs.

Seeking out practical yet good-looking materials from widely available sources does not mean skimping on quality. Standard builders' merchants stock includes basic but honest stainless-steel sinks and white ceramic tiles.

A chunky shelf made from reclaimed pine, painted in tough white eggshell and fitted with new brackets at eye level provides easy access to key cooking utensils and plain china. Beneath this is a metal pole – bought from a builders' merchants, cut with a hacksaw and attached with hanging rail fixings – with butchers' hooks for hanging scissors, colanders, graters and other essential equipment; an idea borrowed from restaurant kitchens.

The wall above is painted in white vinyl silk emulsion, a waterproof surface from which it is easier to remove cooking stains than an ordinary matt emulsion.

The wooden blockboard worktop is practical and tactile, it can be bought by the metre and fitted using screws. Rather than being solid, blockboard is made up of many small pieces of wood moulded together. To keep worktops in good order, sand before use and seal with several coats of wood sealer. If any black mould marks appear, simply repeat the process every few months.

retro style

VILLAGE-HALL GREENS AND BLUES, JUNK KITCHEN CHAIRS AND SPOTTY FABRICS CREATE A FRESH TAKE ON THE VINTAGE LOOK.

My grandmother's kitchen houses a large dresser spilling with stacks of plates and cup hooks hung with tattered recipes, tea towels and dog leads. How homely and reassuring. It is no wonder that the retro look is so appealing to the frazzled twenty-first-century homemaker.

The kitchen in my own home was once the domain of Betty: she prepared the daily tea at 4pm on the dot, with trays spread with starched white linen and wholesome cakes. This is a peaceful, productive room, so I chose a soft green colour in eggshell that echoes the past yet at the same time looks contemporary. Colour is key to creating a nostalgic mood (think sludgy greens, creams, eau-de-nil and grey). The texture of the colour is important too, with matt chalky surfaces looking more old-fashioned. The colour is used as a device to unify the walls and the furniture – the dresser and cupboards are painted in eggshell whilst the walls are in emulsion.

To get the dresser look, you can make do with a robust freestanding metre-high wooden cupboard with drawers (look in junk yards for old school and office furniture and the bases of dressers that have been separated from their shelves). Put up rows of shelves above and paint all the pieces in the same colour for a unified effect.

Furniture and accessories all help to create the retro feel. Painted junk chairs are exactly right for a vintage flavour. Sanding and painting woodwork is a bargain way to update any down-at-heel chairs. Do check, though, for tiny woodworm holes in the wood. Do not buy any item if it is riddled, or treat with a woodworm preparation if there are only a few. Look out for striped, checked, spotted and pretty floral fabrics to make up into chair covers, simple curtains and cloths. Use plain white china and tableware or seek out authentic retro green and cream tinware. (I find the stacking biscuit tins very useful.) The staple kitchenware of wartime Britain often appears in junk shops and on market stalls.

paint problems?

PARTICLES IN THE PAINT: Caused by dust or inadequate wiping down after sanding. To remedy, rub the paint down with a fine-grade wet and dry sandpaper once dry and apply a fresh coat.

DRIPS AND RUNS: Caused by overloading the paintbrush and not spreading the paint out far enough. To remedy, follow the instructions given above.

BLISTERS: Caused by water vapour from damp present before painting or that crept into the wood after. Not noticeable in cold weather, but in heat the water evaporates and blisters appear. When only a few blisters, remove and fill, rub down and repaint surface. If there are too many, start again.

WRINKLES: A crinkled effect that occurs when gloss paint is applied too thickly or to a badly prepared surface. Strip off, sand and repaint.

FLAKING: If flakes occur in new paint, the surface was badly prepared. If flakes occur in old paint, it can be caused by rot due to damp, frost or hot sun. Strip off, prepare and repaint.

ingredients

* Walls painted in soft green emulsion
* Simple wooden dresser painted in soft green eggshell
* Wooden floorboards sanded and painted in white floor paint
* Junk kitchen chairs sanded and painted in powder blue eggshell
* Tablecloth in spot-print cotton (see page 144)
* Spotty apron (see page 130)
* 1940s green and creamware picked up from market stalls

cook's kitchen

STAINLESS STEEL IS AS MUCH AT HOME IN THE DOMESTIC KITCHEN AS IT IS IN THE CATERING ENVIRONMENT.

Such is its strength and practicality, rigorously maintained commercial kitchens are equipped with everything from stainless-steel sinks to cooking pots. On the domestic front, it makes good sense to consider the use of stainless steel for sinks, shelving and worktops.

The highest grade stainless steel is expensive. For a budget option, flick through your local business directory to find suppliers of catering kit from commercial kitchens which have gone bust or are upgrading. Don't be put off that these establishments are usually sited in grimy yards under railway arches, they can be very good sources of sinks and worktops, shelves or stainless-steel fronted catering fridges that can all be put to domestic use.

For something functional without paying a fortune, commission a catering supplier to make a bespoke kitchen. It will be more basic than the average fitted kitchen, but it will be stylishly utilitarian. Here, in the home of a professional pastry chef, one wall of a smallish kitchen has been kitted out with a made-to-order sink, worktop and shelving arrangement in stainless steel.

A key feature of these units is the shallow drawers that allow for the storage of cups and cutlery. As in commercial kitchens, the sink is wide and deep for washing up big pans and stacks of plates. It is possible to increase worktop space in an arrangement like with a custom-made chopping board that rests over the edges of the sink.

Simple triangular brackets support two rows of shelves that hold saucepans, casseroles and a food mixer – the mighty gadget with which Jonny prepares his lemon cakes, iced coffee cakes, gloriously crispy pear tarts and other mouth-watering puddings. Jonny is a lofty individual who has no problem grabbing his gear from the upper shelves. For those who lack inches, however, keeping shelves low so that the most used tools are within arm's reach is more ergonomic.

Recessed halogen downlighters are fitted above the work surface, and there is lino flooring that is maintained with a damp mop and detergent. In order for cooking operations to be carried out efficiently, a gas cooker and wooden preparation table are sited opposite the sink area.

Despite its name, stainless steel can be stained by various substances – salt, acidic food, bleach and some detergents. Wipe down regularly with lemon juice or a cut lemon to brighten the surface. Don't fuss too much about stains they are part of the normal wear and tear.

ingredients

* Walls painted in pale pink vinyl silk emulsion
* Stainless-steel kitchen units and shelving
* Floor covered in creamy yellow lino
* Halogen downlighters over work surface
* Fold-up wooden drainer
* Heavy-based pots and pans to create culinary magic

tip HOW TO LIVE WITH LINO If laying sheet lino onto a wood floor, any proud nails must be either pulled out or punched in. An underlay should be laid and stuck in position with lino adhesive. Lino can be bonded to concrete or stone in the same way, providing the floor is clean, dry and level. It is important to seal lino; washing an unsealed lino with hot water and detergent tends to open the pores and remove the oils blended into the lino during manufacture so that it becomes increasingly difficult to clean. Seal with a specialist cleaner for best protection, but wash with detergent before sealing in order to remove the manufacturer's protective film.

country without the chintz

PLAIN TONGUE-AND-GROVE DETAIL, SIMPLE ACCESSORIES AND A BIG WOODEN TABLE ARE THE ESSENTIAL INGREDIENTS FOR THE MODERN COUNTRY KITCHEN.

There are some rustic romantics who can't get enough of the Aga life: laundry slowly drying on the overhead airer, hot bread straight from the oven and steamy dog baskets. If the trad farmhouse feel is not your cup of tea, however, a more modern, pared-down country look is workable whether you're living in the sticks or wedged between a Chinese and a chippy.

There is a simple L-shaped run of kitchen units – the tongue-and-groove detail is country without being twee – with cupboards for storing pots pans, cleaning materials and food, and the obviously practical close arrangement of oven, sink and dishwasher. Also in tongue-and-groove, a basic slimline cupboard with double doors and shelving is wide enough to take the biggest dinner plates (any wider and it would take up too much space and look clumsy). To make the most of the natural light seeping in from the window, the sink is positioned below the window for washing up with a view.

A work surface in unpolished creamy marble fits in comfortably with the natural understated look. Similarly, the tiled terracotta floor – sealed with several coats of linseed oil to repel red wine, olive oil and other cooking culprits – has all the components of country style: rough in texture, earthy in colour and hard-wearing. (Heavy tiles like this are not advisable when the weight-bearing ability of flooring above ground level is an issue.)

The key accessories that bring this simple look together are a solid chestnut table and folding chairs that can also be moved al fresco (the table has a detachable top) when the sun shines, functional glass Kilner jars for storing dry goods and a large metal florists' bucket filled with heady scented tuberoses.

ingredients

* Wooden tongue-and-groove doors and cupboards painted in white eggshell
* Walls painted in white emulsion
* Terracotta-tiled floor
* Marble worksurface
* Open shelving
* Simple glass Kilner jars for storage
* Simple chestnut dining table large enough to seat ten people
* Fold-up wood and metal slatted chairs in white
* Stems of white tuberoses for a summery feel (their heady scent thickens as dusk falls)

tip

HOW TO PUT UP A BASIC SHELF
* Mark the position of the shelf at several points along its length using a spirit level to ensure it is straight and level.
* Drill two 6mm holes in the wall with a masonry drill using two shelf brackets as a guide for positioning.
* Insert 6mm masonry wall plugs into the drilled holes. The plugs should be flush with the wall surface.
* Using four 40mm screws, fix the brackets to the wall.
* Attach the shelf to the brackets using four 32mm panel pins.

crisp blue and white

EAT WELL IN A SIMPLE, UNCLUTTERED, BLUE-AND-WHITE DINING SPACE.

To ensure the important business of eating and drinking is the main focus of meal, the ingredients for my perfect dining room are simple: white walls, white woodwork and simple roller blinds in blue-and-white striped cotton create a blank canvas that serves as the backdrop for the food.

A sanded and waxed wooden floor is not only practical – easily cleaned after a long Sunday lunch or the most boisterous children's tea – but creates a feeling of spaciousness even in small areas.

The simple Shaker-style beech chairs are a sixties' design that is becoming increasingly sought after, so much so that there is now a roaring trade on eBay. I have managed to buy them for a song, however, from ordinary high-street junk shops whose owners were unaware of their collectability.

Blue-and-white cotton checks look fresh, so use a length of fabric to make a simple tablecloth. Or, if you feel your chairs aren't up to scratch, sew your own simple pull-on loose covers.

Set the table with plain white china and simple glassware – elements that will not detract from what delicacies are being served up to eat.

When it's cold and wintry outside, pots of narcissi and amaryllis bought inexpensively from local florists bring spring colour and scent, whilst the shadow-intensifying candlelight softens the mood and inspires conversation.

ingredients

* **Walls painted in white emulsion**
* **Wooden floorboards sanded and waxed**
* **Blue-and-white striped cotton roller blinds**
* **Flatpack pine table painted in undercoat and two coats of white eggshell paint**
* **1960s beech dining chairs**
* **Blue-and-white checked tablecloth**
* **Candles on the table**
* **Amaryllis and narcissi in flower pots**

tip

HOW TO SAND A FLOOR
* Set aside an entire weekend for sanding a floor; don't think you can do it all in a day.
* Move everything out of the room to clear the floor.
* Hire a sander with a drum and an edge sander.
* Level the floor by removing all protruding tacks and hammer any floor nails below the surface.
* Wear goggles and a face mask.
* Always allow the sander to move forward; don't let it stand still.
* Start sanding with a medium-grade paper and finish with fine.
* When sanding, move along the length of the floorboards, never across them.
* Move the edge sander parallel with and close to the skirtings and along the floorboards.
* Vacuum and mop the freshly sanded floor to remove any dust before painting, varnishing or sealing.

sleep

10 WAYS TO MAKE A CALMING BEDROOM

1 Calm colour. I would advise sanity-promoting whites, greys, lavender, soft blues, greens and creams as soothing shades for the bedroom.

2 Soft textures. Goosedown duvets and pillows ensure a good night's kip. For additional warmth, padding and body cosseting why not use a traditional feather bed, which fits between the mattress and bottom sheet.

3 Life is too short to iron bedsheets. Fold while slightly damp and dry on a radiator, folding and refolding, for a few hours or leave to flap dry outside before putting straight onto beds. Annoyingly, pure linen is the easiest fabric to iron, but it is also the most expensive.

4 Comfort underfoot. Early morning feet don't appreciate icy cold surprises. Even if you desire bare ceramic or wooden floors, be kind to your toes with a cotton bedside rug or natural fibre mat.

5 Invest in a decent firm mattress. For back support, try a hand-tufted mattress stuffed with cotton and wool felt. Turn it every few months to prevent it sagging where you sleep. Lay a blanket between the sheet and mattress to protect it and to provide a smooth underside to the bottom sheet. It is also extra toasty in winter.

6 Good things to help you sleep. Lavender pillows stored in the linen cupboard impart their herby scent. Traditional hot water bottles in woolly covers warm sheets in winter. Pillows stuffed with cherry stones warmed in the oven are a different eco-friendly take on the bed warmer.

7 Think big bed. Even if your room's dimensions are limited, a bigger bed gives you a greater surface area to work, rest and play on. If you're bothered about storage, invest in a bed frame with space beneath for boxes and crates to stowaway bedroom clutter.

8 Every bed needs a side table with books, a clock and a small vase of tulips, roses or, perhaps, garden herbs. Bedside lamps trimmed with ribbons and bows are making a comeback; the prettier and girlier the better. See page 150 for a pretty lampshade idea.

9 Good storage. Keep the bedroom clutter free with built-in cupboards and shelves and white boxes stored beneath the bed. A basic hanging rail covered by a white sheet is the tidiest wardrobe solution if you've spent all your money on a set of linen sheets.

10 Poor sleepers benefit from black-out blinds or lined curtains to keep out early morning light. Plain roller or Roman blinds can be pulled down permanently to diffuse the light and afford privacy. White cotton, blue-and-white ticking or floaty muslin drops with ribbon or tab ties are simple to run up on the sewing machine.

attic retreat

USE WHITE TO CREATE LIGHT AND AIRY WRAPAROUND COLOUR.

Attic rooms are a godsend in households where the domestic habits and musical preferences of the teenage members clash with those of their parents.

When considering an attic space as a bedroom option, obviously it is essential to ensure that the roof is well insulated and lined. This can be achieved by covering the space between the battens with strips of roofing felt or polythene, then nailing thermal plasterboard to the battens to form the ceiling. Adequate light is also an issue. It could involve the addition of skylights or a new dormer window construction; this may need planning permission, so check with your Local Authority.

In this snug teen loft space, roof and walls are clad in tongue-and-groove panelling – boat-shed style – in keeping with the oarsman activities of the sixteen-year-old resident who on the nearby river. As part of a general overhaul of the roof, extra light has been punched in, here, with a new double-glazed Velux window, an off-the peg purchase that is relatively cheap to buy and have installed.

Painting the entire space white, using eggshell on the walls and ceiling and specialist floor paint on the floor boards, is not only a stylistic consideration, but it is also effective at making the space appear much lighter in view of its low levels of natural light.

Then there is the issue of the loadbearing capability of an attic floor. To prevent a fast descent through to the rooms below it will be necessary, for example, to lay new floor timbers on the joists if the existing floor is made of only thin hardboard. This is an area which a good builder should be competent to advise on.

ingredients

* Walls clad in pine tongue-and-groove panelling painted in white eggshell
* Wooden floorboards sanded and painted in white floor paint
* Swedish style wooden bed
* Blue-and-white striped bedlinen
* Bedroom chair with pull-on washable calico cover with button detail
* Washable white cotton rag rug

tip

HOW TO PREPARE WOODWORK
* Wash all woodwork down with water and a little detergent.
* If stripping damaged or flaking paint, use a blowlamp (cheap but a fire risk), a hot-air gun- heavy (safer and better for large areas) or a chemical stripper (expensive and noxious but good for small areas and mouldings - there are solvent, caustic and peel-off varieties).
* Fill all holes and cracks with wood filler.
* Sand and then treat with a wood primer after rubbing down.

spare and calm

FREE YOUR SLEEP SPACE AND YOUR HEAD WITH CLEVER STORAGE SOLUTIONS.

One of my many unruly habits, along with slicing bread unevenly, is not putting my clothes away so that by the end of the week there is an enormous heap draped over the bedroom chair. Tidying this lot up slices into my cherished Saturday lie-in time, tucked up with toast and strong coffee. But at least I am very lucky to have decent wardrobe space in which to decant the chaos.

When my bedroom is uncluttered it is such a freeing place to be, and one in which I can think more clearly when trying to keep early morning worries from spiralling out of proportion.

The room has two alcoves either side of fireplace and so the solution of two fitted cupboards was an obvious one. But rather than deep cupboards, which visually intrude more, they are quite slim (just 45cm deep), with hanging rails fitted at right angles to the back walls so that clothes can be hung comfortably. We used 2.5cm thick chipboard for the frame and doors, and 1cm to plant as a simple moulding on the doors. Once painted with an undercoat and three coats of eggshell no one could guess that this is chipboard rather than wood. Above the cupboard there is shelf space that, when I get round to it, I will fill with my favourite Spanish baskets to make extra storage.

Other useful ideas include those fabric hangers with pockets that are good for stashing away knickers, ties and smaller accessories. Low wooden benches make the most of space below – so that you can have several vertical rows for shoes. To keep moths from breakfasting on your favourite woollies, I suggest investing in stout plastic clothes covers and to hang pieces of fragrant cedar wood – an eco moth deterrent – inside wardrobes.

ingredients

* Built-in cupboards sanded and painted in white eggshell
* Wooden floorboards sanded and painted in white floor paint
* Curtain pole painted white
* Tie curtain in blue-and-white ticking (see page 146)
* White cotton roller blind
* White chair covers
* Patchwork cushion

tip

HOW TO PAINT WOODWORK
* Prime any new or stripped wood. Use knotting to paint the knots in soft wood like pine before priming. Use an aluminium primer for exterior soft wood, wood stripped by the blowlamp, hardwood, stained wood and wood with preservative.
* Fill all cracks and holes with wood filler and rub down before priming.
* Combined primers and undercoats are available, which mean you can dispense with the undercoat stage and go straight on to covering the wood with one to two layers of topcoat.

modern florals

KEY GUEST ROOM DETAILS ARE SPLASHES OF COLOUR AND NURTURING TEXTURES.

Papering walls is no longer a hanging offence, so what's to stop you decorating one wall with a fabulous floral wallpaper. It will add colour and detail without going over the top. Big patterns often work really well in small spaces, such as a guest bedroom, where pink roses gallop across the walls without looking in the least bit grannyish.

The secret is to mix in other fresh and contemporary elements, such as a basic bed base or divan – this is not the place for elaborately padded and grand headboards – dressed in a hip pink trimmed sheet and cosy dyed purple cotton blanket. More splashes of modern colour could include a roller blind trimmed with lime green velvet ribbon, a lamp decorated with pink matador bobbles and a dressing table wearing a floaty pink and white skirt.

As well as pleasing colours, the comfort factor is a key detail when it comes to making your guests feel nurtured and spoilt. Crisp cotton sheets and layers of woolly blankets will deal with their immediate needs. There should also be adequate space for hanging up clothes, a bedside table and a small armchair dressed in a pretty loose cover, and maybe a table for working at or doing make-up.

Flowers are always cheering when you stumble in from a punishing journey – not a huge vaseful but perhaps a glass with three or four tulips or just one gorgeous rose. These plus the warm glow from a bedside lamp, a jug of water, a few books and fresh white towels will do perfectly.

If the room hasn't been used for a while do remember to open the open the windows and give it a good airing for a few hours. In winter make sure the heating is on in advance to make it toasty for your arrivals.

ingredients

* Walls papered in floral wallpaper
* Table sanded and painted with voile skirt (see page 126)
* Roman blinds edged with green ribbon
* White cotton bedsheets dyed pink (see page 148)
* Dyed cotton blanket (see also page 148)
* Bedside lamp trimmed with pink bobbles (see page 150)

tip

TIPS FOR WALLPAPERING

* Check every roll of paper has the same batch number, that there are no variations in colour and no faults.
* Walls to be papered should be clean, firm and dry.
* Rub down any paint on walls with sandpaper.
* Scrape powdery or flaky areas and paint with size, leaving them to dry completely.
* Leave new plaster to dry out for six months before papering.
* If walls are uneven, line with lining paper and leave up to 12 hours to dry before papering.
* Some paper needs to be left with the paste on it for a period of time before hanging to allow the paste to soak into the paper and to prevent air bubbles.

bed heaven

NATURAL TEXTURES AND GARDEN GREENS ARE SOOTHING BEDROOM ELEMENTS.

Soft bean green is a soothing, non-confrontational colour idea to decorate with in the bedroom. In this pretty bedroom, filled with early morning summer light, lighter and darker tones of the same colour sourced from a standard paint chart have been washed over the walls in emulsion and in a tough durable eggshell finish to update a Shaker-style flat-pack wooden four-poster.

This natural, from-the-vegetable-garden green makes white bedlinen look crisp and punchy and is also an undemanding backdrop for accentuating colourful accessories and bedside flowers. Using other natural textures such as rough seagrass matting, and a bunch of bedside flowers stuffed in a basic drinking glass helps to complete a harmonious and understated sleep sanctuary.

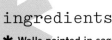

ingredients

* Walls painted in sage green emulsion

* Terracotta tiled floor

* Floor covered with a seagrass mat

* Wooden four-poster bed sanded and painted

* Painted junk chair sanded and painted

* Flexible thirties-style metal light

* Bedside light

* Lavender water cologne to freshen the bedsheets

more handy paint pointers

* During work breaks, wrap paintbrushes or rollers in newspaper or cling film.
* Over night, put paintbrushes in water or brush cleaner as directed on the can.
* Suspend the brush so it is not resting on its bristles and the water doesn't reach the metal parts. Ideally make a hole in the handle, push a skewer through this and balance it on the rim of a jam-jar half filled with water. Shake and wipe before beginning painting the next day.
* At the end of a job, wipe the paint off on newspaper, wash with water or cleaner. Rinse in warm water and leave to dry.
* Wash emulsion paint off a roller until the water runs clear. Wrap in newspaper and squeeze out any excess water. If painting with an oil-based paint, wipe the surplus on newspaper and use the appropriate cleaner. Leave to dry.
* Neglected brushes can be revived. Place the bristles in a pan with a little boiled vinegar and simmer for 30 minutes. Wash in a detergent solution, rinse and shake dry.

girly boudoir

A BEDROOM SHOULD BE A HAVEN OF PEACE AND TRANQUILLITY, WITH NO HARSH OVERHEAD LIGHTING. THE ALL-IMPORTANT COMFORT FACTOR MEANS THAT GOOD FIRM MATTRESSES AND CRISP, COTTON BEDLINEN ARE ESSENTIAL.

Escaping to a bedroom haven is a pleasant diversion from the day's drudgeries, preferably in the company of a yummy box of chocolate and a gripping read. My ideal modern-day boudoir is rather more pared down than a Rococo version spilling with satin and lace, but nonetheless enticing.

Your boudoir can be as compact or as spacious as your needs and space limitations dictate. Even a small box room can accommodate a divan that can be appropriately dressed and draped. What is important, however, is how you introduce an element of prettiness. A colour scheme based on mint green walls and soft rosy pink details is bright, light and suitably girly. The bed should be romantic, with a tented harem feel.

Traditionally shaped metal bed frames look good, especially if you paint them in a rosy pink colour. If the frame is already painted, sand, apply an undercoat and finish with two layers of matt eggshell for durability.

ingredients

* Walls in mint green emulsion
* Nylon mosquito nets
* Simple folding and slatted table
* Pleated paper lampshade
* Pretty printed cotton bedlinen
* Simple metal beds painted in soft pink eggshell
* A box of chocolate violet creams and a good book

Give the same colour treatment to pleated paper lampshades with a couple of coats of emulsion. The paintbrush can also be applied to small bedside tables – a simple folding slatted wooden table normally found in garden departments looks stylish. Apply one coat of all-purpose primer and finish with two coats of eggshell. Use white, as too much pink detail may overdo the effect.

Flowing and diaphanous drapes made from filmy nylon can be hung from the ceiling on a circular frame, which are both easy to find and inexpensive. To hang them, screw a hook into the ceiling, ideally into a joist as the net should not be load bearing. This is a wise deterrent against small children and any cats who might wish to practise their climbing skills. For those who aren't familiar with them, a net like this is a very useful defence against mosquitoes on hot steamy nights.

Make the bed with pretty girly cotton duvet covers or sheets patterned with a retro pink and green floral print. To achieve the maximum princess feel, layer with as many pillows and cushions as you desire.

tip

PAINT PREP
* Before painting, remove any small items, including furniture, lamps, curtains and books, to another room.
* Place any larger pieces in the centre of the room and cover with a dust sheet. Protect any flooring.
* Remove the handles from the doors and window frames.
* Next, prepare all the surfaces that are to be painted in the correct sequence: ceilings first, then walls and lastly wood- and metalwork. Do not skimp on this part. You'll be amazed at how long a pro takes to prepare a room for painting and how short a time it takes to execute the paint job itself.
* See page 18 for more details on decorating preparation.

make the difference

> 66dress your bed in fresh new linens for a simple bedroom update99

sleep tight

The simplest way to change the mood in a bedroom without a complete redecorating job is with a change of sheets, blankets and covers. But remember to choose patterns that look okay with the rest of your bedroom; the look will jar if you're a minimal girl and your bed is bursting with flowery swirls, for example.

In summer, white cotton or linen sheets, and light creamy wool or cotton blankets are cooling and help you to survive the most sweltering temperatures. The bottom sheet should be the best you can afford – ideally 100 percent Egyptian cotton with a 200 thread count. If you hanker after pure linen, buy it old from markets as it will be cheaper and often superior quality.

Fresh blue-and-white seaside cotton stripes teamed with pale indigo sheets are also good summer bedding ideas and not hard to source.

As winter draws in, it's time to think about tucking up with more blankets and cosy textures. Try old-fashioned brushed sheets in pyjama striped pinks or blues – grown-ups appreciate them as much as small people.

Blankets are back, so go hunting at markets and auctions or ask elderly aunties if they have any stashed away in their airing cupboards. Natural fibres last longer when it comes to blankets, too. Take a large mortgage out for cashmere, slightly less for mixing it with lambswool or go for a pure wool cellular version.

Keep snug with the addition of a quilt, which is as varied as its usurper the duvet – duck feather or down, goose down or real eiderdown, which costs thousands. Junk shops and markets are the best places for pretty faded paisley and floral eiderdowns. Lay them on a radiator to freshen up or, better still, air them outside in the sunshine.

wash

10 WAYS TO MAKE A PAMPERING BATHROOM

1 Prioritise. Make a room plan on graph paper (see page 16). Discuss the costs with a plumber before going ahead; it might be worth making a saving on a basic bath so you can invest in a good boiler for on-tap hot water.

2 Cotton textures and great scents. Buy white cotton towels, bath mats and robes (all machine washable) along with good soaps and lotions. I adore black Magno soap by La Toja from the supermarket in Spain.

3 Wipe-down surfaces. Stone, wood, cork and rubber are all good. Avoid carpet and natural sisal as they rot. Use bath mats to soak up water on floorboards. Choose matt surfaces for floor tiles or you will slip.

4 Cotton roller and Roman blinds, half curtains and opaque glass all give privacy.

5 Heat. Install a heated towel rail and in a very small space consider a slim, tall wall-mounted design. Underfloor heating is a really good choice for the bathroom, particularly under heat-retaining ceramic surfaces.

6 Thermostatic showers allow you to control the temperature of the water safely. For concealed shower pipes you need to insert the plumbing before the tiles are put in place.

7 Waterproof paint textures repel moisture. Use vinyl silk or a quick-drying moisture-resistant eggshell finish.

8 Think eco. Showers save the 25 litres used in the average bath. Remember though that a 10-minute power shower uses more water than a bath. Consider solar power to heat water, particularly if you live in southern latitudes.

9 If you can't afford to start again, update what you have; give floorboards a fresh coat of paint and replace tired looking bath tiles with new ones. Streamline your bathing space by boxing in fixtures and fittings with tongue-and-groove panelling.

10 Check your water pressure. A decent shower needs an adequate flow. Use a pressurised system, where water is taken straight from the mains. Depending on the efficiency of your boiler, a pump may be needed to increase the pressure. Low-pressure systems rely on a water tank, but don't deliver a strong flow. Seek a plumber's advice.

simple style

CREATE A SNUG WHITE BATHROOM WITH TONGUE-AND-GROOVE PANELLING.

Boxing in baths, wash basins and unsightly plumbing is a useful way to streamline the bathroom. It can be achieved using various devices such as tiling or wood panelling. Interiors guru Katrin Cargill has gone one step further in her London terraced house: this girl's heart lies in the mountains, so she has kitted out her entire bathroom log cabin-style using lengths of tongue-and-groove to line plastered walls and to box in all the pipework. All of the materials used were quite cheap and the costs were further reduced by using simple mouldings for the skirtings and shelf edges.

Durable white eggshell paint gives the walls a good matt look as well as a tough water-resistant coating.

The traditional-look roll-top cast-iron bath is just the right sort of roly-poly shape to gently envelop the bottom and back during a long hot soak. Stern beauty editors might disapprove of this practice (too drying on the skin) but most of us would admit that the sheer body-reviving sensation of warmth and weightlessness is worth it after a long working day.

On the subject of cast-iron baths, it should be noted that they are extremely weighty and you should check up on the strength of your floor before installing. If you need to remove an old beaten up one it's much easier to break it up on site with a sledgehammer – I know because we did this at home and so saved the bother of hiring some muscle to heave it down the stairs.

ingredients

* **Walls clad in pine tongue-and-groove panelling painted in white eggshell**

* **Wooden floorboards sanded and painted in white floor paint**

* **Free-standing roll-top bath with ball-and-claw feet**

* **Integrated chrome bath taps and showerhead**

* **Pretty gathered half curtain in blue-and-white spot-print cotton**

* **Fluffy cotton bath mat to soak up any drips**

tip

DEALING WITH PAINT SPILLS
* Move fast, ideally deal with any spills the moment they happen.
* Remove emulsion paint splashes from floors with a damp rag while the paint is still wet. Once dried, spots are difficult to budge, but should respond to rubbing with fine wire wool dipped in soapy water. Follow the grain of the wood, use very little water, rinse well and rub dry.
* Remove emulsion stains on fabric with a sponge dipped in cold water. If the fabric permits, leave the stained material to soak in cold water, then wash in the normal way.
* Sponge oil-based paint stains with white spirit or a substitute.
* Spilt paint on a wood or stone floor can be removed if dealt with immediately. Use a brush, spoon or newspaper to quickly get up as much as you can. Then throw dry sand or garden earth on to the stain and scrub hard with broom. On a stone floor, rub in all directions. On a wooden floor, brush the way of the grain only. Sweep up the sand or earth. If any stain remains wash with washing soda dissolved in hot water.
* Paint splashes on windows can be removed by rubbing with a cloth dipped in hot vinegar.

hot water and white towels

TEXTURE AND WARMTH ARE ESSENTIALS IN THE SIMPLE BATHROOM.

If you're planning a new bathroom and money is tight, the golden rule is to aim for simplicity. Resist the urge for a hi-tech, all-spraying-and-steaming shower system or the beautiful but pricey hand-baked Moroccan tiles, as seen in the latest interiors magazine. The good news is that it's possible to buy basic bathroom kit at your local builders' merchant without forsaking style. Thus body and soul can be soothed and cleansed without going into the red.

I followed this route when furnishing our simple family bathroom. With five family members plus the occasional lodger, I knew that our utmost priority was hot water, and lots of it, at any time, so I purchased a mega-flow condensing boiler that was fitted downstairs in the utility room. Although a significant part of the budget was taken

ingredients

* **Walls painted in white vinyl silk emulsion**
* **Walls part-tiled in white square ceramic tiles**
* **Wooden floorboards sanded and painted in white floor paint**
* **Bath boxed in with tongue-and-groove panelling**
* **Integrated chrome mixer tap with hand-held showerhead**
* **Chair covered in white towelling (see page 122)**
* **White cotton roman blind**
* **Worn wooden bath holder and wire soap dish**
* **Fluffy white cotton towels**

tip

TILE TIPS

* Nail battens to the wall at right angles to form the framework in which to start tiling. Check the battens are level with a spirit level.
* Spread adhesive over 1sqm and put the first tile in position.
* Place tiles in horizontal rows, pressing into position and checking they are level.
* Insert spacers between each tile (matchsticks will do).
* Remove battens and spacers when all the whole tiles have been laid and the adhesive is set.
* Cut and fit any remaining tiles. Hold the tile to be cut back to front in the space to be fitted. Mark with a pencil. Turn the tile over, then score with a tile cutter and a steel ruler. Put a matchstick at both edges of the tile under the scored line. Press on both edges to snap it.
* Apply grout in the tile spaces with a sponge when the adhesive is set.
* Run a wet finger along the grout lines for a smooth finish. Clean the surface with a cloth when grout is dry.

up by this beast, I had enough left over to buy a white bath, sink and toilet. A word of warning though, any twiddly details or faux features look tacky on cheap bath kits, so choose the plainest and most honest-looking designs.

Luke, our polish carpenter, made a cradle to support the enamelled steel bath and then boxed it in with tongue-and-groove pine panelling. We then used 6cm square basic white tiles around the bath – also from the same source – and painted the walls in white vinyl silk emulsion that has a good waterproof texture.

From a salvage yard I bought a utilitarian thirties' chrome heated towel radiator taken from an old hotel, which makes damp towels warm and crisply dry. The latter are also sales' buys – half the price because they're seconds – but the odd pulled thread hardly notices.

A chair cover made up from a towel is a simple and comfortable bathroom detail. (see page 122 for a simple pull-on chair cover idea.) Underfoot there are wooden floorboards painted with white floor paint. A cotton bath mat is usually laid to soak up drips, which would otherwise sneak through the cracks in the boards.

simple shower

MAKE A SIMPLE WALK-IN SHOWER USING THE SKILLS OF A GOOD BUILDER, WATERPROOF TEXTURES AND GLEAMING WHITE TILES.

Showering should be as invigorating and refreshing as diving through romping surf. However, the all-too-usual musty shower cubicles that one comes across in cheap flat conversions or local swimming baths induce such feelings of squeamishness that, frankly, I'd rather go unwashed. With its hefty membership fees (my treat to myself), this was not the case at the snazzy city sports club where I'd escape my motherly duties for the regenerating torrents of hot water in sleek glass cubicles.

Could I have my own walk-in wet room at home? Our indefatigable builder claimed he was installing them all the time for his mega-buck clients. But could we do it on a shoestring? 'Leave it to me,' was his reply.

So we ripped out the old fittings from a 3m (10ft) x 1.25m (4ft) bathroom and erected a 1.5m- (5ft-) long floor-to-ceiling stud partition wall to make a walk-in shower cubicle. To the left of the entrance is a heated towel rail and wash basin, and to the right, a built-in cupboard to conceal the shower pipes and to store towels. The stud wall is hung with hooks, behind which lies the door-free shower area.

The bathroom walls and floor were lined with waterproof marine ply – cheaper than other waterproof materials but just as effective – and the floor was raised to make a gentle slope for the water to drain away. We used simple white tiles on the walls that were tanked up to a height of 20cm using three layers of waterproof resin. The shower pipes were concealed in the cupboard behind the thermostatic shower that enables the user to set the temperature of the water and prevent those unexpected scalding or freezing moments – an important factor when children are showering.

On the floor we laid matt mosaic tiles, which are non-slip, that come in 50cm square sheets and so are quick to lay. Both the floor and wall tiles were grouted in an off-white waterproof grout (white discolours quickly and looks dirty against white tiles).

The scheme has been a great success judging by the battle for who gets in there first thing in the morning, and cost-effective, too. To remove lime and mineral deposits from a showerhead, unscrew it and place in a pot with a mixture of equal parts white vinegar and water. Bring the mixture to the boil and the deposits should come off.

ingredients
* **Walls in white ceramic tiles finished with an off-white grout**
* **Floor in white ceramic sheet mosaic tiles, also finished with an off-white grout**
* **Thermostatically controlled shower and simple watering-can style chrome showerhead**
* **Simple downlighter**

tip

TILE TROUBLESHOOTING
* Before tiling, plaster fill cracks and holes, paint with plaster primer.
* Remove any emulsion paint from walls before tiling.
* Remove any wallpaper from walls before tiling.
* Use a flexible tile adhesive when applying tiles to hardboard, chipboard and ply sheets.
* If tiling over an existing tiled surface, rub it down with sandpaper and wash before starting.

by the seaside

WATERY BLUE HUES ARE GREAT FOR A FRESH LOOK IN THE BATHROOM.

The notion of dressing a bathroom in watery hues is a cliché, but blue is such a deliciously evocative colour – whether it conjures up an eau-de-nil sea, a cool blue loch or a lone swimmer at the lido scything through early morning turquoise water – that it is convincing nonetheless. If you're a water bunny at heart, liquid blues can be splashed around the bathroom to make the perfect washroom retreat. Finding the right shade of blue is a process that demands only a paintbrush and a few sample pots of the hues you like most from a colour chart.

I used a rich cobalt blue emulsion from a widely available paint manufacturer to bring a shot of fresh, by-the-seaside colour into our Spanish bathroom. It is a colour that lifts the mood and is a good antidote to dark winter skies (yes, even the Andalucian south suffers from the laden grey skies typically associated with England). Picking out the window frames and mirror in white eggshell adds useful, contrasting colour, which stops the blue look from becoming overpowering.

A victorian towel rail rescued from my grandmother's house is painted in a sea green shade eggshell paint for more seaside-inspired detail.

ingredients

* Walls painted in cobalt blue emulsion
* Woodwork and mirror painted in white eggshell
* Towel rail painted in sea green eggshell
* Fluffy white cotton towels
* Spotlight above basin (check with an electrician before installing)
* Wall-mounted basin with visible waste, looks utilitarian and is space saving

A window flung open to the sunny outdoors creates a lovely feeling of light and spaciousness. Fine for some, but if you're an urban flat-dweller based where space is limited in the bathroom, it is worth using light-reflecting, white tiles and choosing your accessories cleverly: smaller wall-mounted basins or specially shaped ones that fit into awkward corners. Slim, wall-mounted heated towel rails are also good for tight spaces, proving both storage and warmth without taking up valuable floorspace.

---

tip BASIC NOTES FOR FIXING THINGS

You can put up anything from a light frame to a heavy cupboard with the right fittings. Here are some key tips:

✎ nails – choose the correct one for the job in hand. Round or oval for wood, steel for masonry, galvanised and non-ferrous for use outside.

✎ in hard wood, it's easier to insert a nail once a small hole has been made; use a bradawl to make one, then hammer in the nail at a slight angle.

✎ a piece of cardboard or paper can be used to hold a small nail or tack in place whilst it's being hammered.

✎ use masonry nails for fixing light loads like small frames.

✎ screws – most are made of mild steel, but there are also brass, aluminium and stainless steel ones for outdoors.

✎ screwed joints are stronger than nailed ones.

✎ for small screws use a bradawl to make a hole otherwise a drill is usually needed.

✎ drive in the screw with a screwdriver, which fits the head exactly.

✎ use wallplugs or wallanchors and screws for large mirrors, shelves and cupboards.

✎ if walls are not solid, for example partition or lathe and plaster, screw into the stud or joist behind plaster.

make the
difference

**❝Simple ideas
for storing
bathroom kit make a
wash space both
functional and
good to look at❞**

neat and tidy

Inventive storage ideas will enable you to keep your bathroom streamlined and tidy. Here are my favourite storage ideas.

✻ make a roomy drawstring laundry bag in cotton calico and stitch on appliqué flowers (see the appliqué cushion on page 128 for inspiration). Hang it on the back of the bathroom door and fill with your dirty clothes ready for wash day.

✻ visit a salvage yard to seek out an old heated chrome towel rail. They look smart and utilitarian, whilst keeping your towels warm and crisp. If you can't stand white towels, go for colour; sludgy greens and blues together look good or revive greying white towels by dying them your favourite colour (see page 142).

✻ a rack balanced across the bath is useful for holding soaps and wash cloths. You can choose metal, but I prefer the old-fashioned wooden variety that you can either buy new or look out for well-worn and textural ones in shops or on market stalls specialising in retro accessories.

✻ a peg rail is invaluable for towels, flannels and any other hanging kit. Use simple painted wood ones or something in chrome if you want to look more modern.

✻ a stacking trolley, such as a plastic vegetable rack, is a multi-purpose idea and great for storing bath-time accessories.

✻ plain white ceramic beakers are smart and simple for teeth-brushing gear.

✻ use blue-and-white enamelled tin plates from a camping shop for utilitarian and stylish soap dishes.

✻ recycle pretty bottles. Olive oil bottles are rather lovely to decant your favourite cologne into – mine is Gotas de oro, a spicy citrus scent that I buy in spain.

✻ simple open shelving is useful for storing kit above the wash basin.

✻ a lockable wall-mounted cupboard will prevent small people from experimenting with the family's medical supplies.

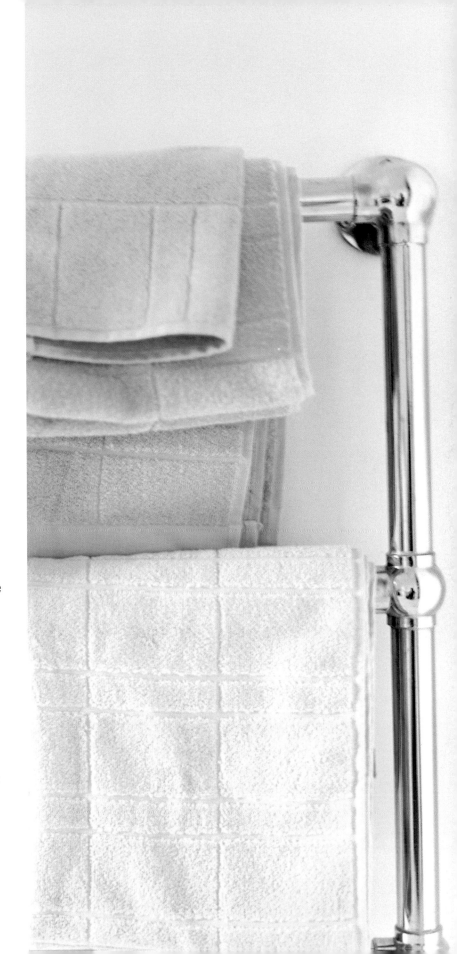

work

10 WAYS TO MAKE A HARDWORKING HOME

 1 Room with a view. Work by a window to make the most of natural light and keep in touch with your surroundings.

 2 Task lighting. Anglepoise lamps are cheap and practical work lighting. White or retro-style metal ones are the best looking.

 3 Utility space for washing, drying and ironing. Even if it's a pokey space, it's better to close the door on laundry than have it draped around the house.

 4 Open shelves for books and boxes to file household papers, cuttings and research material. You can never have too many.

 5 What to do with rubbish? Recycle plastic, metal and paper at your local depot or use the special recycling bags that a growing number of local authorities now provide. For general household use choose a bin that will contain at least 40 litres.

 6 Cast your eye around junkyards and second-hand shops for old work tables, office chairs and filing cabinets to update with a lick of paint.

 7 If cupboard space is limited, buy plastic crates that stack on top of each other to store diy tools and any painting kit. Don't hang on to dregs of paint as it goes off quickly. Take any almost-empty cans to your local rubbish tip.

 8 Decorate with whites and neutrals – peaceful and undemanding colours to work in.

 9 Eco-office. Recycle old computer equipment, save envelopes for re-use and use recycled papers for writing on.

 10 Eco-utility. Cut down on harsh household chemicals like bleach. Half a cup of baking power in the machine with a liquid detergent revives whites in a wash. Use vinegar and water to clean everything from tiles to windows. Save newspapers for covering surfaces when doing DIY and polishing shoes.

on the shelf

SIMPLE FURNITURE AND PRACTICAL STORAGE ARE ESSENTIAL FOR A CALM AND ORDERED WORKSPACE, PROVIDING THE PERFECT BLANK CANVAS FOR INSPIRATIONAL MOOD BOARDS.

To maximise the use of available space, employ a decent carpenter to build shelves as tall as your ceiling height allows. Since you will have to pay for labour and materials, this will turn out to be more expensive than buying freestanding shelving, but crucially size and shape is tailored to suit your particular needs.

I would suggest using chipboard to at least cut down on the cost of materials. Cheaper than solid wood, it is made up of small chips of soft wood bound with glue – like an inedible flapjack mix – which is squeezed between rollers to make smooth sheets of the required thickness. Plus points: it has an even texture and is resistant to warping. Downsides: it bows if support is inadequate, the cut edges may be uneven and special screws are needed for fixing.

An alcove kitted out with shelves in this manner is a brilliant space saver. Snugly supported with a central spine, these shelves are 75cm (2ft 6in) wide, 26cm (10in) deep and 35cm (14in) tall to fit most magazines and box files. Tip: for narrow books like paperbacks, fit a false back to the bookcase to make a narrower shelf.

For efficiency, stack the tallest books at the bottom, together with boxes of paints, work folders and work bags. Remember to have a sturdy stepladder at hand for reaching the higher shelves.

ingredients

* Walls painted in white emulsion
* Chipboard shelves painted in white eggshell
* Junk table painted in white eggshell
* White card file boxes bought as flatpacks
* Cork tile pinboard (see page 116)
* Table lamp with cream parchment shade

tip

HOW TO PAINT FLOORBOARDS

* For the smoothest finish, sand the floorboards with an industrial sander (see page 60).
* Vacuum and mop the floorboards and leave to dry.
* Apply one coat of primer/undercoat with a paintbrush and leave to dry for time stated on tin.
* Floor paint is particularly sticky, so it is wise to wear rubber gloves whilst applying it with a paintbrush.
* Apply the first coat of floor paint following the length of the boards. Leave to dry for up to 12 hours or the time stated on tin.
* Apply a second coat. Some floor paint takes several days to become really hard so it is wise to keep the space empty until then.
* Floor paint is pretty hard-wearing but it does scratch. Consider a re-paint after a year or so, but remember that with each re-paint the flat smooth look will not be so apparent.
* Keep the painted floorboards clean with a mop, hot water and detergent.
* If boards have been painted in white floor paint, break the eco-rules every now and then and wash with water and bleach to bring back the whiteness.
* If there isn't the budget for an industrial sander then you can simply clean the boards and hand sand, before applying layers of undercoat and paint. The finish will not be as even, however, and so less pleasing aesthetically, and the boards will be harder to keep clean.

make the difference

basic utility storage

Built-in cupboards are an investment as you will need to employ a carpenter. Costs can be reduced by using cheaper materials, such as MDF or pine, to make the cupboard frames and doors.

Plan your space carefully and make a sketch with accurate measurements (see pages 16–17 for an example). Think about the size of the objects that you want to store, including those things that are used less frequently as well as those items that you need to grab every day.

If plumbing is involved, consider the siting of the waste – it will be an important factor if it is a distance from your planned site.

> "Built-in cupboards are the simplest and most space-saving method of storing the clutter of domestic life"

CLOSED: Doors: tongue-and-groove wooden doors have been primed and undercoated, then finished with two coats of oil-based eggshell paint. Simple handles have been painted white to keep the wall of storage uninterrupted. Baskets: traditional rustic baskets are both utilitarian and textural – what better way to carry a bundle of washing out to dry

OPEN: Shelves: layers of shelves provide storage for towels and linens. Slatted shelves help the air to circulate and keep linens free from damp. Solid shelves store an iron and cleaning materials. Cupboards: a narrow cupboard houses an ironing board, fold-away clothes airer and loo rolls and provides a hide away for the washing machine, with space above for a basket of laundry.

so easy

DRESS UP A WORK NICHE WITH PRETTY PAPER AND PRINTS.

Even if your nest is spatially challenged, and you have sacrificed the spare room for a child, a lodger, or a partner who is easier to live with if they have their own bolthole, find a niche, even if it's tucked in the corner for your work and creative musings. Make it pretty and personal and you're bound to feel more inclined to get down to business.

See here where pale powder blue wallpaper in an old-fashioned floral contrasts with a junk-purchase desk, contemporary floor light and painted frames with black-and-white photos to create a fresh and eclectic workspace.

If a small area can't contain the tools of your trade, earmark shelves or cupboards elsewhere in the house (I have borrowed what was the old built-in linen cupboard at the top of the house to house my collection of fabric lengths and remnants). If this isn't a possibility, buy cheap stacking boxes or drawers in white plastic or card to keep things neat and tidy.

Similarly, a small desk will cope with a laptop or basic sewing machine, say, but if you need more space for laying things out, consider trestle tables with separate painted mdf tops that can be folded away if you need to use the space for something more pressing. There's nothing wrong with the floor for cutting out dress patterns or laying out presentations.

ingredients

* **Walls papered in powder blue floral wallpaper**
* **Painted frames with ribbon detail (see page 138)**
* **Junk table**
* **Chair covered in pull-on loose cover (see page 122)**
* **Floorlamp for pools of soft light**
* **Flexible work task lighting**

tip

REMEDIES FOR WALLPAPER PROBLEMS

TEARS: Cheap papers tear and are difficult to hang, so use mid-price ones. Perhaps paper only one wall if money is tight. The wallpaper will also tear if is left to soak too long.
UNSTICKING: Damp walls and too little paste can stop paper sticking. Press edges of paper with a cloth or seam roller to make sure they stick.
MISMATCHING PATTERN: If the pattern doesn't match it is usually due to irregular stretching because the strips have been soaked for varying times.
BUBBLES: Lumpy paste and insufficient brushing out will cause bubbles. If wet, lift the paper and smooth out. If dry, cut a cross at the centre of the bubble and stick down the flaps.

work hard

A SIMPLE UTILITY SPACE MAKES LIGHT OF DOMESTIC CHORES

I wouldn't give up the larder, a proper walk-in one with shelving for all our food, but I dispensed with a second bathroom to allow for utility space. I find it efficient and calming on the mind to be able to do the laundry and ironing in a separate room – a necessity at home where I run the Ritz of suburbia and there are always vast piles of washing to process.

It isn't a big space – about 3m by 1.5m – but it's just large enough to iron and listen to the Archers in peace; and to accommodate a worktop and sink with space below for a washing machine and laundry basket.

I'd strongly recommend a ceramic butler's sink (from ordinary building supply shops). They come in various permutations but the deep ones are very useful for washing things like oven trays, muddy dogs, paint pots, and hand wash-only stuff. They must sit on some sort of support – either a chrome base with legs or a cupboard unit that can be used to store cleaning materials.

If you arm yourself with a spirit level, it's not too irksome to put up a simple shelf with brackets (see page 58). Paint in white eggshell for a tough wipeable finish.

Similarly a wood worktop should also be sanded and sealed with two coats of a clear eco-friendly wood sealant. Use fold up clothes airers if you don't have a dryer – the old-fashioned wood ones that concertina into a flat shape are much more sturdy than most plastic or metal ones. Best of all, if you have a garden and it's clement weather, dry everything outside on a washing line.

ingredients

* Walls painted in white vinyl silk emulsion
* Wall below shelf painted in blackboard paint
* Worktop in block board
* Ceramic butler's sink on built-in chipboard cupboard
* Open shelving for storage
* Storage pots made from recycled plastic (see page 120)
* Fold-up laundry basket
* Pretty pinny for looking glam whilst doing the chores

tip

HOW TO UNBLOCK A SINK

Household debris, kitchen waste and hair are the most likely reasons for a sink to be blocked. Try to deal with it yourself before calling out an expensive plumber. Have you got a rubber sink plunger? No, well go and get one from the hardware store. Place it over the plughole and pump it up and down a dozen times. Pull off the plunger to break the seal with the sink. Repeat this until the water empties. If this doesn't work, remove the trap or open the access plug. Place a bucket under the outlet pipe before opening and use a piece of wire or cane to clear the pipes on either side of the trap. If the waste doesn't drain, the blockage is beyond the trap. Hire a metal snake or clearing rod to investigate further, but at this stage, you're likely to need a plumber. Avoid using harsh chemicals, such as caustic soda.

study area

MAKE A SIMPLE FOLD-DOWN DESK TO HELP YOU WORK, REST AND PLAY

If you're proficient with a saw and electric drill, why not make your own fold-down work desk. It can be easily stashed away when it's time to play or chill out.

Start by screwing a length of 7.5cm (3in) by 5cm (2in) timber securely to the wall, placing the timber so that the top edge is approximately 75cm (30in) above the floor. Using two 5cm (2in) by 5cm (2in) hinges, screw the desk legs to the underside of the desk top – a piece of 2.5cm (1in) thick chipboard measuring 120cm (48in) by 60cm (24in). To ensure that the desk will lie flat when it is folded down against the wall, fix one leg 5cm (2in) further from the front edge than the other. Congratulate yourself that you have got this far and take a break.

Now, with a friend in tow (more hands make light work), you need to screw three 10cm (4in) by 5cm (2in) hinges to the back edges of the underside of desk top. Your friend can help line up the desk top with the timber baton while you screw the other side of the hinges into place.

Now you have the perfect surface on which to exercise your studies. If like me, you are an expert in displacement activity, leave the brain work a little while longer and give your handiwork the finishing touches by sanding, priming, undercoating and finally painting the desk with two top coats of eggshell.

ingredients

* Walls painted in white and red stripes
* DIY fold-down desk in wood and chipboard
* Sofa bed covered in pink cotton corduroy
* Patchwork Liberty print cotton and canvas cushions (see page 128)
* Floorboards painted in white floor paint

tip

FLOORBOARD FLAWS?
SQUEAKING OR LOOSE BOARDS: Tighten the boards so that they don't move by screwing the boards on to the joists. For extra firmness, hammer in extra brads and sink the heads below the surface with a nail punch.
GAPS BETWEEN BOARDS: This happens when there is shrinkage due to central heating or splintering due to rot. Replace any really damaged boards with new ones. Small gaps can be lived with and a few large ones can be filled with strips of wood made level with the surface, but any floor riddled with gaps would benefit from being covered with hardboard. If you have the patience and money, the whole lot could, of course, be lifted and relaid.

garden

10 WAYS TO MAKE AN OUTDOOR ROOM

 **Plan:** treat your outside space like an interior room with sketches, colours, textures and list of plants that you like.

 Short cuts: paint peasticks and make your own wigwams for quick-growing climbers, like clematis and climbing roses. Buy herbs such as rosemary, lavender and box in bulk – much cheaper – to plant as pretty hedges.

 Dig. Get your soil turned and composted and import some new topsoil, if necessary. It's worth paying for some muscle.

 Decking is going down. Overexposed as a result of TV garden makeover shows, decking is out of favour and not really justified unless you live by the sea or have a roof terrace or an area where heavier materials are not suitable.

 As long as you punch holes for drainage, plants can be grown in almost anything: plastic bowls, old sinks, wooden tubs, metal buckets. The key is to feed and water plants regularly. My favourites are leggy lilac or white agapanthus, which both thrive when packed together in terracotta pots.

 Cover ugly surfaces with a lick of paint. In colours: matt pea green and organic sludgy blues and greys. Out colours: harsh wood stains in electric blue and white gloss finishes.

 **Inspiration:** my heroes are David Hicks for his pragmatic garden design, Gertrude Jekyll for her practical advice, Joy Larkcom for her salad growing tips and for great advice, Gardeners' Question Time on Radio 4.

 A soft, springy lawn. Spread with inches of topsoil before treading down and re-seeding. To maintain good drainage, spike every autumn with a fork and brush in topsoil and sand. The growth of lawn grasses combined with regular mowing will keep weeds under control.

 Natural textures: old bricks laid in herringbone patterns to edge borders or make pathways; terracotta placed in a chequer board pattern; a line of old flags; gravel pathways; sturdy canvas and thick cotton.

 Look in second-hand shops for garden furniture; there are often simple benches and folding chairs. Garden tables can be improvised using salvaged doors and a couple of trestles. Then there are basic but perfectly acceptable all-in-one picnic benches with seating – dead cheap and more stylish once painted.

dig it

GROW GOOD THINGS IN YOUR GARDEN, INCLUDING VEGETABLES FROM ORGANIC SEED AND LOCAL VARIETIES.

Dig a vegetable plot in the garden or if you're a flat dweller take on an allotment to grow organic food. (Allotments are owned by local councils and if there's a waiting list in your area you can approach nearby councils about vacancies.) Digging in plenty of compost is the key to rich, nourishing soil from which you will be able to grow succulent and proper tasting produce.

Either buy-in compost or better still, build a compost heap. Contain it within brick or concrete blocks or planks of fencing with ventilation holes.

Place sticks or other coarse material at the bottom to let the air in. Use leaves, vegetable waste, wood shavings, eggshells, lawn cuttings, tea bags, and build in layers. Water the heap and once built cover with earth and a lid to keep the heat in and speed the rotting process. By building a second compost head alongside the first, the organic gardener will find that the first has rotted down.

Border the vegetable patch with utilitarian paths made from planks of wood, see right, old bricks, broken shells, pebbles, gravel and old bricks. Or you could try pretty edgings using herbs like mint, chives, and parsley, or hazel sticks bent to make scalloped edges. I recycled Victorian terracotta ridged edgings from the front garden to make simple boundaries for my new vegetable and flower plot that will hopefully start to show the fruits of our winter labours later on this year. I am growing beans and tomatoes up wigwams made from peasticks, together with rows of onions, lettuces, potatoes, courgettes, spinach and rocket. I am keen to plant blackcurrants, too, for compotes, jams and summer puddings.

ingredients

* Good compost from a compost heap
* Good things to grow, especially organic seeds
* Peasticks to train beans and tomatoes
* A large sun hat

tip

HOW TO MAKE A PEASTICK WIGWAM

* Not only do they add height in the garden but wigwams built from peasticks (canes) are brilliant for training up beans tomatoes, sweetpeas and other cottage garden climbers.
* Peasticks are sold in hardware shops and garden centres, and are very cheap. They come in various lengths, but I'd go for one that will allow 180cm (6ft) feet plus 30cm (12in) that will be pushed in the earth to keep the structure sturdy. Remember to allow an extra foot to be pushed into the soil.
* To construct take six sticks, bunch them together and bind from 5cm (2in) below the top with lengths of raffia to make a 5cm (2in) wide band.
* Splay the sticks out wigwam fashion and push into the ground.
* Three or four wigwams in a row look good, or position 4 at each corner of a vegetable patch.
* Paint the canes in a garden green emulsion colour to look stylish.
* Don't treat a wigwam as a permanent fixture as it will rot naturally after a year or two.
* Consider other materials such as lengths of cut hazel for organic looking and woody wigwams.

potted garden

PUNCH A HOLE IN THE BOTTOM OF ALMOST ANY CONTAINER TO FILL WITH SOIL, WATER, FEED AND WATCH THE GARDEN BLOOMS GROW.

The paved terrace outside Mandy Bonnell's kitchen door (also see her retreat on page 108) becomes a blaze of colour when the contents of her bucket containers are in full bloom. For someone who had 'bulbs growing upside down four years ago' Miss Bonnell has come a long way with her gardening self-education supplied by plant guides and the pearls of TV gardening gurus. Now she knows how to pierce the bottom of a bucket with a bradawl, throw in stones or brick pieces for drainage and fill with a good compost to make the perfect growing medium. In spring she has tulips, fritillaries and narcissi (all planted the right way up), which are supplanted later by nicotiana, poppies and good things to eat such as basil, and tomatoes (San Marzano, the Italian plum variety). For year-round greenery there is a huge pompom privet, 'my extravagance, but much cheaper than box'. Mandy clips it twice a year, in May and August, to keep it in shape.

ingredients

* Walls painted in off-white emulsion (re-done yearly)
* Fifties pale blue and white buckets from junk shops and local markets
* Pompom privet grown in an old metal dustbin
* Simple white folding metal table and wooden chairs

tip

HOW TO PAINT POTS

Machine-made terracotta pots can look a bit too perfect so it is a good idea to give them a bit of textural colour for a more weathered look. I make a wash of emulsion (watering it down with an equal amount of water for a thin consistency) in whatever colour suits the garden – I usually use white for our cool patio in Spain and a soft bean green for our London back garden. Before painting, simply clean the pot and wipe off any dirt. Either apply one coat of thinned emulsion for a washed-out look or add another coat if want more defined colour. Leave to dry for at least one hour before planting.

colour in the garden

MAKE THE DIFFERENCE IN THE GARDEN WITH A FRESH LICK OF PAINT.

The little garden shed was in a sorry state, gently rotting at the bottom of the garden, until it was given a facelift with pale powder blue eggshell on the windows and door and a soft bean green shade in a couple of coats of oil-based undercoat.

The great thing about paint is that you can use it to add style and colour to your outside space, even if it's a garden in its infancy or the most basic balcony. Use it to embellish elements such as furniture, trellis, to unify patched runs of fencing and to revive a worn-out shed.

The key is to use understated colours that look organic and natural. Sludgy blues and greens look gorgeous against borders with summer pinks. White always looks fresh and perky for details like New England-style picket fences. Bright lime greens, sky blue, yellows, oranges are strictly for tropical surroundings.

Tough specialist outdoor finishes can be costly but there are ways to cheat and save money, such as using interior matt emulsion on walls if you don't mind doing a yearly re-paint. The soft green colour I so desired for my fence came from an expensive range of outdoor stains, but I took a shortcut by matching the pigment by computer at a paint shop and had it added to an oil-based undercoat that looks great and is tough and weather repelling

Important: when painting metal furniture, use a rust-proofing undercoat and then an oil-based undercoat with a top coat or eggshell. Gloss paint gives too much of the shine factor.

ingredients

* Shed walls painted in soft bean green oil-based undercoat
* Shed windows painted in powder blue eggshell

smart shed ideas

* Paint the interior walls white for a light and bright seaside look or a soft garden green or blue.
* Fit out your shed with shelves and paint them in the same colour. Use them to store all your garden kit.
* Fix simple hooks to the walls so that you can hang up everything from your hand garden apron to a net bag of spring bulbs.
* Stick to bare floorboards that can be given a good scrub; they are the most practical floor surface
* Collect wooden crates from your greengrocer or garden centre to use for storage. You could even paint them.
* Keep a couple of deckchairs and a fold-up table in your shed. Spread with a tablecloth and decorate with lanterns or hurricane lamps for a romantic retreat or summer picnic.

pint- sized urban retreat

A FORMAL GARDEN SHAPE WITH INFORMAL PLANTING IDEAS.

Print maker Mandy Bonnell's tranquil garden, a stone's throw from thundering city traffic, was an overgrown mound when she started work on it just three and a half years ago.

The plan: to create a formal shape – echoing the proportions of her Georgian terraced home – with an informal array of cottage garden plants. Working with elbow grease, shovels and a wheelbarrow Mandy re-arranged the existing gravel to make box-edged paths which wrap around a central bed bordered with flagstones and 'little lottie' dwarf lavenders.

Filling up her tiny garden is Mandy's passion, and, as she is without a car, she depends on mail-order bulbs and seeds from cottage garden plant specialists.

On the north-facing back wall, there are shade-loving specimens: an early flowering Montana clematis, climbing hydrangea, ferns and hostas. On the side walls, Mandy cultivates phlox, deep red sunflowers, aquilegias, dahlias (cut down and protected under flower pots over winter), campanula, standard roses and a quince tree. The central bed is packed with leggy alliums, a gorgeous 'raspberry ripple' iris and gladioli (a much maligned plant in the upper echelons of garden design).

ingredients

* Gravel and flagstone paths
* Old brick walls
* Beds edged in box and dwarf lavender
* An array of cottage garden blooms
* Shade-loving plants for a north-facing wall
* White painted wood and metal bench

tip

HOW TO LAY A BRICK OR GRAVEL PATH

* Work out a plan before you start.
* It's worth employing a builder (check that he is experienced in outdoor works) or a garden designer (probably much more expensive) for this sort of heavy work.
* Patios and paths need a firm base if they are not to sink into the ground.
* The ground should be levelled as much as possible beforehand.
* A layer of ballast should be shovelled on, then a layer of cement to make a hard level surface on which to lay bricks, stone or gravel.
* Drainage is important so the surface should slope gently towards a drain.
* Old weathered bricks look great in herringbone and other brick- wall tiled patterns. Don't have flush pointing as it looks very nasty – the brickie won't like it but ask for it to be below the level of the brick – fill the remaining space with silver sand.
* Old flagstones are beautiful, but they are costly.
* Consider gravel – by far the cheapest option and available in various colours, sizes and textures. Otherwise, shingle is a very good material to suit most situations.

cool white patio

MAKE A ROOM OUTSIDE IN SUMMER.

At the start of the summer holidays in Spain, I put on my spattered pinstripe painting shirt and pink cowboy scarf to repaint the greying exterior walls in our patio garden. Up here in the hills after the heavy winter rains, it is a necessary task. The traditional way is to use lime wash – but as it's a time consuming business mixing it all up, I'm afraid that I head for the local paint shop to buy tubs of matt to do the job, quickly and cheaply. Hell, I want to get out there in the sun! One coat is enough to make it all look fresh.

Out come the garden tables; having been stored inside they don't need attending to. Next I rig up my outdoor lighting system of lanterns strung along the wall. By day we sit under a blue and white striped cotton awning, which is stretched across the yard. At night it's rolled back to reveal the stars as we feast on goodies from the bbq and summer salads.

Try this idiot-proof idea for roast vegetables: Slice chunks (about 1cm/½in thick) courgettes, aubergines, onions, tomatoes, peppers and garlic gloves. Put in a shallow roasting dish. Sprinkle with 2–3 tablespoons olive oil and a few sprigs of thyme and rosemary. Cook at 150°C for 45 minutes or so, turning occasionally, until soft and crisp. Feast on sardines grilled on the fire, plates of roast vegetables and something ice-cold to drink.

✳ ingredients

✱ **Walls painted in white emulsion**

✱ **Table painted in eggshell**

✱ **Cushions and cloth in cotton fabrics**

✱ **Glass holders for candles**

✱ **Metal lanterns**

tip

SHADY BUSINESS

Make an awning to give cooling shade to an outdoor patio by stretching an extra large piece of canvas from one wall or fence to another.

✱ Look out for extra wide widths of canvas. These are best found at hardware specialists. The wider the canvas, the better, so you don't have to sew too many pieces together to get the spread.

✱ Fix as many hooks, all at an equal distance, along each wall or fence as necessary. Depending on the boundary wall or fence, aim to place the hooks at a height of approximately 2.3m (7ft 8in).

✱ Hem any raw edges on the canvas, making sure it is large enough to give the spread needed.

✱ Stitch pairs of 10cm (4in) long pieces of cotton tape along the length of the canvas to to match up with the hooks on the wall and use these to fix the awning in place.

PART 3

20 things to make and do

potato-cut print

THE HUMBLE POTATO IS A MOST USEFUL TOOL FOR CREATING A SIMPLE POLKA DOT PRINT.
SIMPLY LOAD A CUT SPUD WITH PAINT TO MAKE A PRETTY SPOT DESIGN.

If you want random spots, simply apply them at will. However, for a more regular pattern, mark out equidistant rows using a pencil and long measuring tape. Someone to hold the tape will make the process quicker.

STEP 1. Simply cut the roundest potato you have in half. Mould it into shape with a knife if it's not quite as circular as you want – don't worry about it being perfect, the charm of this technique is its handmade irregular quality.

STEP 2. Pour the paint – emulsion is good – into a paint kettle or bowl and dip the potato in. Don't overload it or the paint shape will splodge and run when applied to the wall.

STEP 3. Stamp the potato cut firmly on the wall to make the spot shape and repeat if not defined enough.

STEP 4. Allow to dry for about an hour, step back and admire your handiwork.

"Soft pistachio green painted polka dots give a sweet yet contemporary wall finish"

cork tile pinboard

PIN-UP IMAGES TO INSPIRE YOUR CREATIVE FLOW. PAINT THE PINBOARD IN A PALE POWDER BLUE OR SIMILAR SUBTLE SHADE TO LET OTHER COLOURS SING THROUGH.

When gluing the tiles to the wall surface, make sure you press the cork tiles down very firmly as they can lift away from the wall. If the wall is slightly uneven or the tiles are going to be painted, I recommend using the tile supplier's own brand of water-based glue.

STEP 1. Mark out your desired dimensions of the pinboard onto your wall surface. My pinboard is seven tiles high and five tiles wide. If you have an awkward space to fill, don't worry – just cut the tiles to size.

STEP 2. It is most important that the wall surface is clean; wash it down with sugar soap and leave to dry before applying the tiles.

STEP 3. Check your measurements carefully, then stick the cork tiles to the wall surface following the manufacturer's instructions.

STEP 4. Leave the tiles for approximately 24 hours to allow the glue to dry thoroughly. Once the glue is dry, paint the tiles with two or three coats of emulsion.

materials

To make one pinboard approximately 210cm x 150cm:

* **35 cork tiles, approximately 30cm square**
* **Tape measure**
* **Pencil**
* **Water-based glue**
* **Emulsion**
* **Paintbrush**

painted wall stripes

WANT MORE COLOUR IN YOUR LIFE? MAKE A BOLD STATEMENT WITH WIDE PINK AND WHITE PAINTED STRIPES.

materials

* Newspaper or dustsheet
* Extending tape measure
* Low-tack masking tape
* Pencil
* Large paintbrush
* Paint tray or kettle
* Emulsion in two contrasting colours

When painting in the stripes, use one coat of emulsion if you want to see the brush marks or, if you prefer a solid colour, add a second coat.

STEP 1. Thoroughly prepare the surface to be painted (see pages 13 and 73). Make sure the wall is free from any dirt and dust. Mask off all plug sockets, skirting boards, floor edges and where the wall meets the ceiling using low-tack masking tape. Put down the newspaper or dustsheet. Paint the wall that is to be decorated with a base coat using one colour emulsion. Allow paint to dry.

STEP 2. Measure the width of the freshly painted wall and mark the centre with a pencil. Working from the centre point of the wall, measure 15cm either side of this point and mark. This will form the central vertical contrasting stripe.

STEP 3. Mask off this first stripe from floor to ceiling with the low-tack masking tape, placing the tape on the outside edges of the pencil marks. Check the vertical lines are straight using the spirit level.

STEP 4. Continue masking off 30cm wide vertical stripes across the rest of the wall, but remember to place the masking tape for every alternate red stripe on the outside edge (therefore just inside the border of the white stripes). When the entire wall is masked off, paint in the centre and alternate stripes using the red emulsion paint taking care to stay within the masked lines. Once painted, slowly and carefully peel off the masking tape to reveal the design. Allow paint to dry.

1 & 2. Measure centre of wall and mark out first central stripe in pencil.

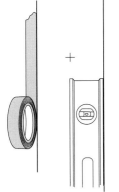

3. Mask off central stripe on outside edges and check with spirit level.

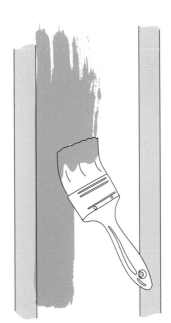

4. Mask off stripes across entire wall, paint alternate stripes in contrasting colour. Peel away tape and allow to dry.

painted plastic pots

GET INTO ECO MODE AND RE-INVENT PLASTIC WATER BOTTLES, CREAM CARTONS AND YOGHURT POTS AS SIMPLE STORAGE CONTAINERS.

Paint the insides of the pots, too, to make them look more finished – a paler or darker shade of the outside colour looks very effective.

STEP 1. Empty and rinse out the plastic bottles, making sure they are thoroughly clean and dry.

STEP 2. Cut the tops of the bottles off to give the required size and shape.

STEP 3. Place the bottles onto the newspaper. Paint the cut-down bottles with two or three coats of emulsion, allowing the paint to dry between each coat, until the plastic is perfectly covered.

materials

* Selection of plastic bottles and pots
* Sharp scissors or craft knife
* Newspaper
* Paintbrush
* Emulsion

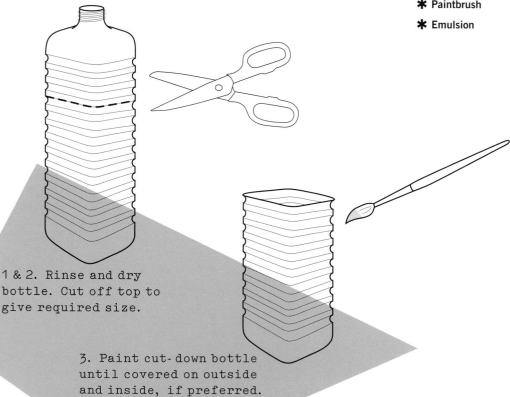

1 & 2. Rinse and dry bottle. Cut off top to give required size.

3. Paint cut-down bottle until covered on outside and inside, if preferred.

easy couture chair cover

DRESS UP PLAIN KITCHEN CHAIRS WITH PRETTY PULL-ON GINGHAM COVERS, CUT AND TAILORED TO FIT FROM A SINGLE PIECE OF FABRIC.

Budget-priced but pretty and washable, cotton gingham is a good choice for a crisp and modern look.

STEP 1.   Measure the chair to be covered. Use newspaper to make a template. Trace the lines of chair front and back, and the chair seat, adding seam allowances on each side. Include a drop from the seat, again plus seam allowances. It is possible to create a chair cover from one piece of fabric, but you will need leave generous 7.5cm seam allowances.

STEP 2.   Lay the material out flat and cut out the pattern template. Make the cuts in the material as shown on the artwork so that the chair cover can be fitted at the seat corners. Do not cut the sides until you are sure that they are in the right place.

STEP 3.   Stitch the back and front together, down to the point where the chair back meets the chair seat, leave the rest free.

STEP 4.   Now hem all the raw edges around the drop to make the chair skirt. Fit over your chair and relax.

materials

* **Fabric, such as lightweight gingham cotton**
* **Tape measure**
* **Sharp scissors**
* **Sewing thread**
* **Dressmaker's pins**

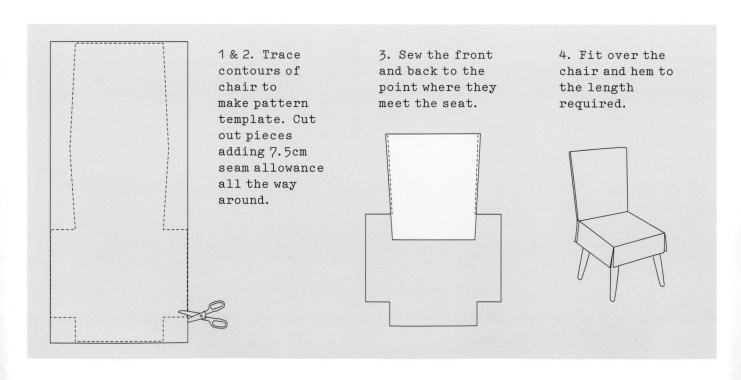

1 & 2. Trace contours of chair to make pattern template. Cut out pieces adding 7.5cm seam allowance all the way around.

3. Sew the front and back to the point where they meet the seat.

4. Fit over the chair and hem to the length required.

painted junk table

WITH GOOD PREPARATION, EVEN THE SCRUFFIEST JUNK ITEM CAN BE GIVEN A SMART NEW LOOK WITH A COUPLE OF COATS OF PAINT.

Use an oil-based eggshell finish to make your table more resilient.

STEP 1. Place the your chosen item of junk-shop wooden furniture on top of some sheets of newspaper or a dustsheet. Sand down the wood using medium-grain sandpaper, working along the grain rather than across it. Wipe down the table with a damp cloth to make sure it is free from any dirt or dust.

STEP 2. Paint the entire table with one coat of combined undercoat/primer. Start with table top and move down the legs following the grain of the wood. Allow to dry. If the wood grain still shows through, apply another coat.

STEP 3. When the undercoat is dry, apply two coats of oil-based eggshell following the same painting sequence for a good even finish.

"I find that my best
junk buys are both
functional and simple
in shape**"**

curtained dressing table

STORE YOUR JEWELS AND TRINKETS ON A PRETTY PAINTED DRESSING TABLE HUNG WITH A LIGHTWEIGHT FILMY SKIRT.

Using muslin or a similar lightweight fabric for the skirt will let the light through and look exceptionally pretty.

STEP 1. Follow all three steps given in the instructions for the Painted Junk Table on page 124.

STEP 2. Measure the perimeter edges of the front and sides of the table to calculate the amount of fabric you will need. The length of your curtain is up to you. Mark out the measurements of the fabric, allowing 1cm seam allowance all the way around, plus 3cm hem allowance along the top and bottom edges. Cut out the fabric.

STEP 3. Turn and stitch a 1cm hem along all side of the fabric. Turn and stitch a 3cm hem along the top side of the curtain to make a pocket through which the tape can be threaded. Turn and stitch a 3cm hem along the bottom edge.

STEP 4. Attach the ribbon to the top of the curtain by sewing along the outside edges. Take care not to sew over the fold made for the tape. The ribbon should be about 2cm from the top of the curtain.

STEP 5. Thread the tape through the top pocket of the curtain and pin into position with a drawing pin at the end of each tape (assuming the table is not a priceless Chippendale).

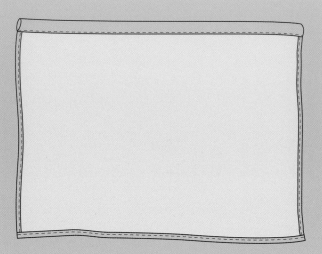

1, 2 & 3. Paint the table. Measure and cut fabric to size. Sew 1cm seams along all four sides. Sew 3cm pocket along the top for tape to be threaded through.

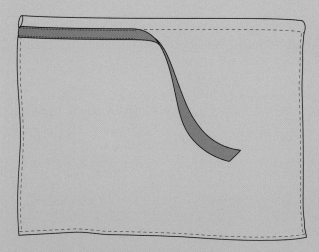

4 & 5. Sew ribbon to top edge. Thread tape through pocket. Pin curtain into position around table.

materials

* Small wooden table with an open front
* Newspaper or dustsheet
* Medium-grain sandpaper
* Undercoat/primer
* Large paintbrush
* White emulsion
* Tape measure
* Lightweight fabric, such as muslin, for curtaining
* Ribbon, approximately 2.5cm wide, for trim
* Cotton tape, approximately 2cm
* Drawing pins

groovy appliqué cushion

NOT SURE WHAT TO DO ON A WET AFTERNOON? CUT OUT PRETTY HIPPY FLORALS FROM LIBERTY PRINT COTTON TO MAKE GROOVY FLOWER-POWER CUSHIONS.

STEP 1.   From the plain fabric, cut two squares to the size of your cushion pad adding 5cm to one side and adding 2.5cm seam allowance all the way around. Turn and stitch a 2.5cm hem on one short side of both pieces.

STEP 2.   Draw a flower shape onto card or stiff paper. Use as a template to cut out flowers shapes from fabric remnants. Leaving the edges raw, pin the cut-out flowers to the right side of the cushion cover pieces, placing them randomly. Hand sew using neat running stitches in coloured thread.

STEP 3.   With right sides together, place the two cushion panels with raw sides edge to edge. Pin or tack together. Stitch 2.5cm seam around the three unhemmed sides.

STEP 4.   Cut eight lengths of the cord, tape or ribbon approximately 20cm long. On each tie, fold one end back neatly and stitch in pairs to both sides of the cover opening at equal intervals. When all eight ties are in place, turn the cover right side out. Insert the cushion pad and tie into bows.

materials

* Plain cotton fabric for cushion cover
* Remnants of patterned fabrics for appliqué
* Card or stiff paper
* Dressmaker's pins
* Sharp scissors
* Cord, linen tape or ribbon for ties
* Cushion pad

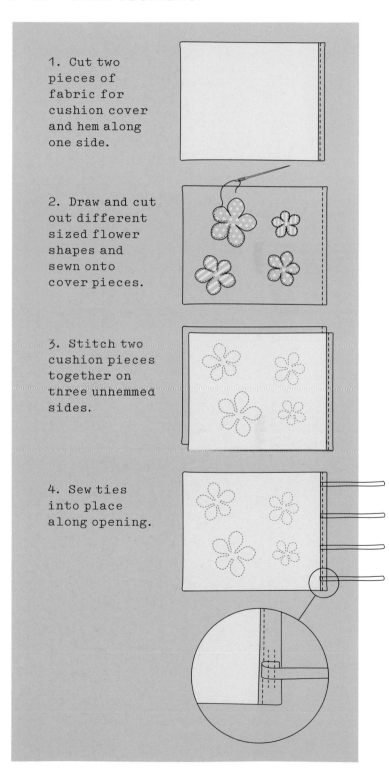

1. Cut two pieces of fabric for cushion cover and hem along one side.

2. Draw and cut out different sized flower shapes and sewn onto cover pieces.

3. Stitch two cushion pieces together on three unhemmed sides.

4. Sew ties into place along opening.

frilly pinny

FOR ANOTHER LOOK, MAKE THE PINNY FROM CREAM CALICO AND TRIM IT WITH A FRILL OF PRETTY FLORAL OR POLKA-DOT PRINT COTTON.

STEP 1. Cut out pattern pieces leaving 2.5cm seam allowances all the way around.

STEP 2. Pin, tack and stitch length of rickrack to sides and shaped edge of apron front (A) approximately 1.5cm in from outside edge.

STEP 3. For the frill, stitch the two short ends of the frill pieces (B) together. Open out the seam and press flat. Turn under 1cm hem along one long side of the frill. Pin and tack. Stitch. Sew two parallel lines of running stitch 1cm from the top edge of the frill and gather it up evenly to measure the same as the curved edge of the pinny front. Secure gathers with a pin.

STEP 4. With right sides facing, align the raw edges of the frill with the sides and curved edge of the pinny front. Pin and tack together. Stitch 1cm in from the edge. Open out the seam and press flat.

STEP 5. For the ties, turn under 1cm hem along all sides of ties (C). Pin and tack. Stitch.

STEP 6. Press and fold in 1cm on all sides of waistband (D). Press and fold in half. Gather top edge of apron A to width of waistband. Secure thread with a figure of eight around a pin. Pin or tack the waistband into place. Slot the ties into the sides and stitch around three open sides.

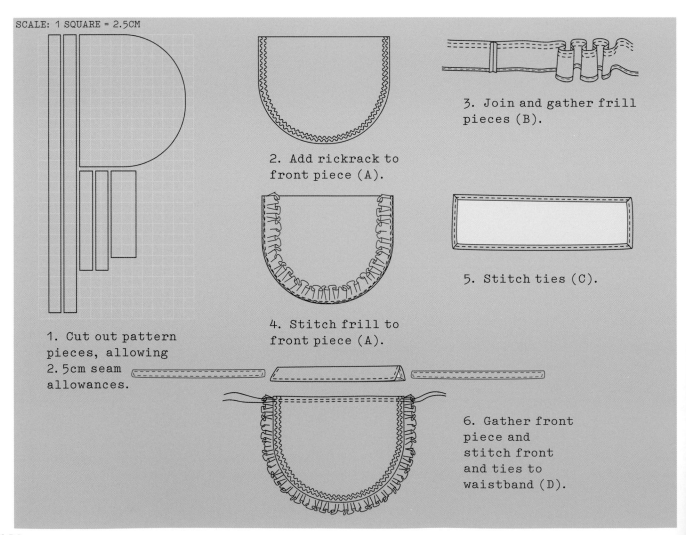

SCALE: 1 SQUARE = 2.5CM

1. Cut out pattern pieces, allowing 2.5cm seam allowances.

2. Add rickrack to front piece (A).

3. Join and gather frill pieces (B).

4. Stitch frill to front piece (A).

5. Stitch ties (C).

6. Gather front piece and stitch front and ties to waistband (D).

materials

* Fabric, such as lightweight gingham cotton
* Sewing thread
* Rickrack
* Sharp scissors
* Dressmakers' pins

easy-care chair cover

STICKY FINGER- AND MUDDY PAW-PRINTS? THIS BASIC LOOSE COVER IN STRIPED TICKING CAN BE THROWN IN THE WASHING MACHINE TO COME OUT LOOKING AS GOOD AS NEW.

Try the cover on the chair as you are making it to avoid any surprises. Do not worry about it being perfectly fitted – a few bags and sags are part of its charm – but to fit the cover more easily around the arm curves, pin and cut as you go. If the chair that you are covering is perfectly symmetrical then you can leave the cover inside out when fitting it over the chair so any adjustments can be made easily. Loose covers need to be laundered. Make sure the cover is large enough to allow for any shrinkage. If necessary, wash a small sample of the fabric to check for shrinkage.

STEP 1. Remove the cushion from the chair. Make templates for individual pieces with newspaper or place fabric directly onto chair following the diagram. Spread the fabric out over a large clean table or floor. Cut out sections of roughly the same sizes as the individual parts of the chair. Remember to allow for seams and hems.

STEP 2. Cut a length of fabric for the inside back of the chair, adding 7.5cm all the way around for seams. Using dressmaker's pins, pin the panel to the chair inside back, wrong side out. Cut a length of fabric for the seat, including the drop at the front and adding 7.5cm all the way around for seams. Pin to the chair, wrong side out. Now pin the panel and the seat on to the large arm panels. Stitch the skirt to the seat and attach the horizontal arm verticals. Finally add the back of back.

STEP 3. Trim off all excess fabric to leave a 2cm seam allowance all the way around. Remove the pins one by one and re-pin the fabric pieces together, making smooth seam lines. Once you have gone over the whole chair, carefully take the cover off. Tack along the pinned edges. Remove the pins and machine. Turn up the hem to the drop required, pin and tack. Stitch. Turn the chair cover right side out. Fit the cover on the chair and pin up the bottom hem, then stitch. Now freshen up your ticking cover with a quick iron.

STEP 4. For the seat cushion cover, cut out two pieces of fabric the size of the seat cushion adding 2cm all the way around for seams. Cut a side panel from the fabric to the same length as the perimeter by the width of the cushion, adding 2cm all the way around for seams.

STEP 5. With the right sides facing, pin, then tack the side to the top panel. Stitch 2cm from the edges, snipping the corners. Attach the bottom panel with the right sides facing, leaving an opening at the back for inserting the cushion pad. Turn right side out. Insert the cushion pad and hand sew the opening with small, neat hand stitches to close.

materials

* **Fabric, such as cotton ticking**
* **Newspaper**
* **Tape measure**
* **Tailors' chalk**
* **Sharp scissors**
* **Dressmaker's pins**
* **Sewing thread**

continued overleaf ☞

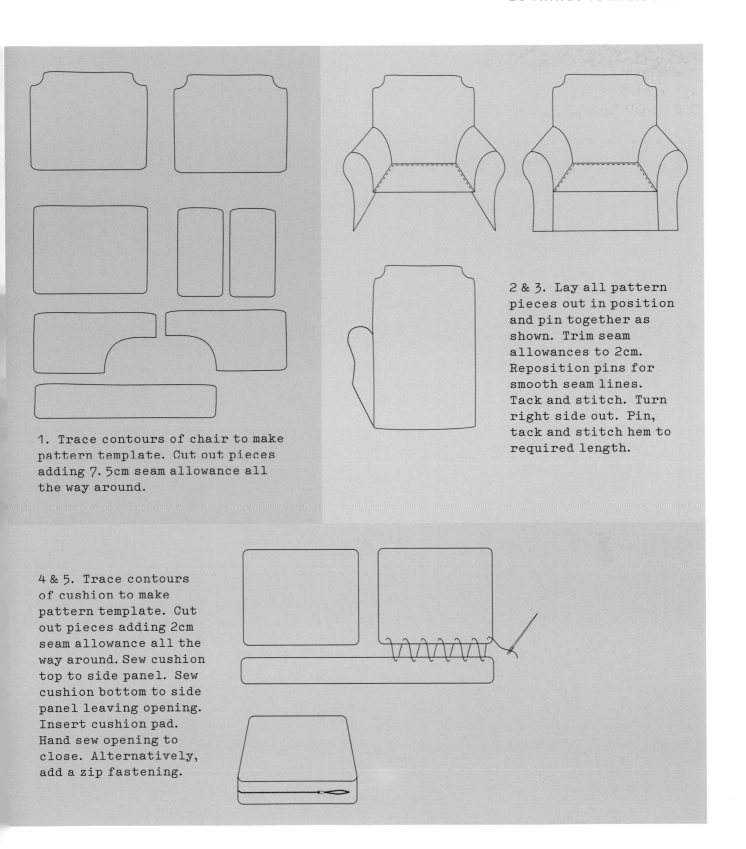

1. Trace contours of chair to make pattern template. Cut out pieces adding 7.5cm seam allowance all the way around.

2 & 3. Lay all pattern pieces out in position and pin together as shown. Trim seam allowances to 2cm. Reposition pins for smooth seam lines. Tack and stitch. Turn right side out. Pin, tack and stitch hem to required length.

4 & 5. Trace contours of cushion to make pattern template. Cut out pieces adding 2cm seam allowance all the way around. Sew cushion top to side panel. Sew cushion bottom to side panel leaving opening. Insert cushion pad. Hand sew opening to close. Alternatively, add a zip fastening.

painted chest

ALL YOU NEED IS A STEADY HAND TO CREATE THE STRIPE OUTLINE ON THIS JUNK-FIND CHEST OR DRAWERS. A STRONG COLOUR, LIKE THIS CORNFLOWER BLUE, GIVES CONTRAST.

When masking off the drawers fronts, make sure the masking tape is pressed well down or the paint will 'bleed' and make your lines look blurred and untidy.

STEP 1. Follow all three steps given in the instructions for the Painted Junk Table on page 124. Remove drawers from chest to paint them otherwise they will become stuck.

STEP 2. Mask off an even border of approximately 2.5cm around the edges of each drawer front using low-tack masking tape. Using a small paintbrush, paint in these borders around each drawer front. For a strong colour, apply two coats of contrasting emulsion.

STEP 3. Once painted, slowly and carefully peel off the masking tape to reveal the design. Allow to dry before replacing the drawers in the chest.

66Simple detail such as this contrasting outline is all that is needed to make a perfectly ordinary chest of drawers look really rather stylish99

ribbon hung frames

MOUNT YOUR FAVOURITE BLACK AND WHITE PHOTOGRAPHS IN PRETTY PAINTED FRAMES AND 'HANG' THEM WITH RIBBON IN THE HOTTEST COLOUR YOU CAN FIND.

The trick here is to nail the ribbon into place first of all and then hang the frames with small masonry nails at appropriate intervals along the lengths of ribbon. Use different sized frames for a more informal look.

STEP 1. Lightly sand down a selection of wooden and plastic junk-shop picture frames using medium-grade sandpaper. Place the frames on sheets of newspaper and paint each one with an undercoat/primer and then two coats of emulsion, allowing each coat to dry. Once the frames are thoroughly dry, mount your favourite pictures and photographs and place them in the painted frames.

STEP 2. Nail a long strip of wide ribbon to the wall where you want the pictures to hang. Cut another length of ribbon about 20cm long and tie into a knot. Nail the knot over the top end of the strip of ribbon, making sure that the nails cannot be seen.

STEP 3. Hang the painted frames over the length of ribbon with gaps of approximately 8–10cm between each frame. Fix into place with small masonry nails, making sure the backs of the picture frames are each equipped with hanging wire.

materials

* Selection of picture frames
* Newspaper
* Undercoat/primer
* Emulsion
* Paintbrush
* Wide ribbon, satin, velvet or cotton
* Scissors
* Small masonry nails
* Hammer

ribbon-tie pillowcase

THIS BASIC PILLOWCASE HAS AN ENVELOPE OPENING WITH TIES. CUSTOMISING THE CASE
WITH RICKRACK AND CONTRASTING RIBBON TIES GIVES IT A SIMPLE AND PRETTY LOOK.

materials

* To make one case for a standard
  size pillow (48cm x 74cm):

* Fabric, such as lightweight cotton
  or linen, 50cm x 1.65m

* Rickrack, 2.2m

* Ribbon, 1.2m

* Sewing thread

* Pillow, 48cm x 74cm

STEP 1. For front (A), cut a piece of fabric to the size of the
pillow adding 1cm seam allowance to each side. For backs (B and
C), cut two pieces of fabric the length but two thirds the width of the
pillow adding 1cm seam allowance to each side.

STEP 2. Cut a length of rickrack to the perimeter of front (A).
Turning under the ends of the rickrack where they meet, pin, tack
and stitch it just inside the outer edge of right side of front (A).
Lay backs (B and C) right sides down and turn in a double 1cm hem
on one short side of each. Pin, tack and stitch. Press. With right
sides together, lay backs (B and C) over the front (A) with raw sides
edge to edge so that the two seamed edges overlap.
Pin or tack together 1cm from edges. Stitch.

STEP 3. Turn right side out. Press. For the ties, cut six lengths of
ribbon 20cm long. Fold under 2cm at one end of each tie and pin in
place, evenly spaced across the opening, in pairs with one either side
of the opening. Hand stitch each ribbon in position taking care not to
sew through more than one layer of fabric.

STEP 4. Insert pillow into case and tie ribbons to enclose.

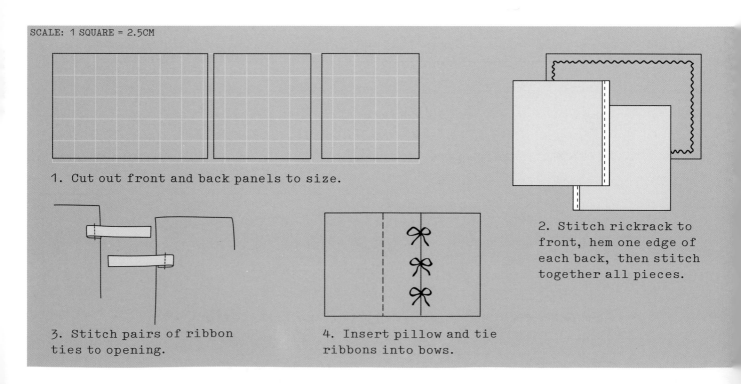

SCALE: 1 SQUARE = 2.5CM

1. Cut out front and back panels to size.

2. Stitch rickrack to
front, hem one edge of
each back, then stitch
together all pieces.

3. Stitch pairs of ribbon
ties to opening.

4. Insert pillow and tie
ribbons into bows.

custom-dyed towels

GIVE A NEW LEASE OF LIFE TO TIRED-OUT TOWELS BY DYEING THEM IN PRETTY SHADES OF PINK AND LAVENDER AND ADDING HANDY HANGING TABS.

For best results when dyeing at home, pour the dye and salt directly into the machine drum and place the damp towels on top. Do not try to dye too many items at once. Remember to wash the dyed towels separately the first time you use them.

STEP 1. Weigh your towels to calculate how much fabric dye is needed. Check the quantities given on the packet instructions. One packet will dye up to 500g dry weight fabric. Dyeing larger amounts of fabric will result in a lighter colour. Place your chosen towels into the washing machine and wash them on a quick-wash cycle to make sure they are perfectly clean before dyeing. Even if towels are new, they must be washed to remove any fabric dressing that will prevent the dye being taken up. Remove the towels from the machine but leave damp.

STEP 2. Wearing rubber gloves, empty the fabric dye directly into the drum of the washing machine. Do not place the dye into the soap dispenser or a dispenser ball. Add the salt on top of the fabric dye. Place the damp towels back into the machine. Wash the towels on a 60°C colourfast cotton wash cycle without a pre-wash or according to the packet instructions. When the wash cycle has finished, add washing powder and run through the hottest possible programme for the fabric, preferably 95°C. Remove the newly dyed towels and hang up to dry away from direct heat or sunlight. If the final wash cycle was below 95°C, wash the dyed towels separately for the first couple of washes to remove any excess dye.

STEP 3. To make the hanging tab, fold a piece of ribbon approximately 15cm long in half and stitch the open ends together to make a loop. Stitch the sewn ends of the ribbon securely on to one corner of the towel.

materials

* Selection of old towels
* Rubber gloves
* Machine fabric dye
* 500g salt
* Gingham ribbon, approximately 2.5cm wide

tea towel tablecloth

IF YOU DON'T WANT TO USE TEA TOWELS, STITCH TOGETHER A PATCHWORK OF CHECKS, STRIPES AND FLORALS CUT FROM VINTAGE CURTAINS AND CUSHIONS.

materials

* Tea towels or assorted remnants of fabric
* Sewing thread
* Bias binding or ribbon for edging, 6cm wide

STEP 1.   Pin then tack the tea towels together with 1cm seam allowance to achieve the size of tablecloth required. Stitch. Open out the seams and press flat.

STEP 2.   For the edging, cut two strips the length of opposite sides of the tablecloth plus 2cm. With right sides together, lay the edging strip along the edge of the tablecloth with raw sides edge to edge. Pin and tack into place. Stitch 1cm from the edge.

STEP 3.   Bring the edging strip round to the reverse side of the tablecloth, turning under 1cm. Pin and hand sew in place.

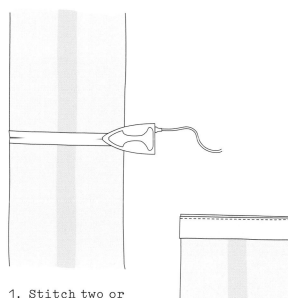

1. Stitch two or more cloths together. Press seams flat.

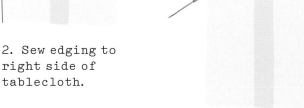

2. Sew edging to right side of tablecloth.

3. Fold edging and hand sew to wrong side of tablecloth.

ticking curtain

TIE-ON LOOPS ARE THE SIMPLEST WAY TO MAKE A BASIC CURTAIN.

STEP 1. Cut out all the curtain pieces as shown, making sure that the long sides of the curtain tops (A) and (B) are the same measurement as the width of the curtain panels (C) and (D), adding 2.5cm seam allowance all the way around.

STEP 2. With right sides together, align the raw edges of one long side of a curtain top (A) to one short side of a curtain panel (C). Pin and tack together. Stitch 2.5cm in from the edge. Open out the seam and press flat.

STEP 3. Turn under a 2.5cm hem along the top and both sides. Pin and stitch taking care at the corners.

STEP 4. On the right side, sew a length of ribbon over the seam where the curtain top and main panel join. Attach with parallel lines of stitching as shown.

STEP 5. Turn under a double 2cm hem along bottom edge of the curtain. Pin and tack in place. Secure with neat hand stitches.

STEP 6. Repeat all steps for the second curtain.

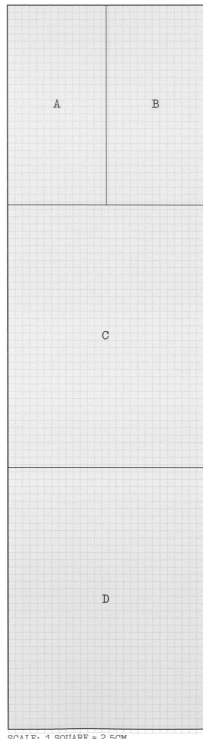

1. Cut out pieces as shown.

SCALE: 1 SQUARE = 2.5CM

materials

* **To make one pair of curtains approximately 325cm x 147cm**
* **5m fabric, such as cotton ticking, 1.5m wide**
* **Sewing thread**
* **8.3m ribbon for trim**
* **2.5m ribbon for ties**

2. Stitch top (A) to panel
(C) with 2.5cm seam.

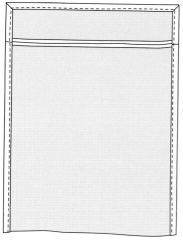

3. Stitch top hem and
side seams.

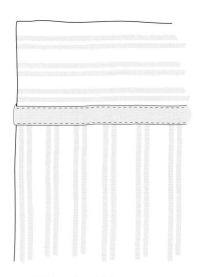

4. Stitch ribbon over seam
to disguise join.

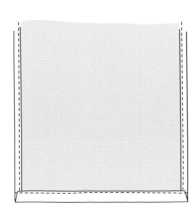

5. Stitch hem.

diy bedlinen with ribbon trim

TUCK UP WITH ONE-OFF BEDLINEN IDEAS: DYED PLAIN COTTON SHEETING IN HOT PINK TRIMMED WITH STRIKING RIBBONS.

Experiment with other trimmings, such as cotton broderie anglaise dyed to your favourite colour.

STEP 1.   Follow steps 1 and 2 of the Custom-dyed Towels on page 143, making sure you rinse out the machine afterwards and taking care to wash the sheet separately at first.

STEP 2.   Sew your chosen lengths of ribbon across the entire width of the sheet at the top edge, stitching along each edge to secure.

materials

* **Double size cotton sheet, approximately 137cm wide**

* **Rubber gloves**

* **Machine fabric dye**

* **500g salt**

* **2.25m each cotton velvet and grosgrain ribbon**

* **Sewing thread**

luscious lampshade

TREAT YOUR LAMPSHADE AS YOU WOULD A FABULOUS HAT AND DECORATE WITH RIBBONS, BOWS AND OTHER SARTORIAL TRIMMINGS.

Make sure the lampshade is the right proportion for the base and also check that the lampshade carrier is the right size.

STEP 1. Place the lampstand on top of newspaper or a dustsheet and sand, working along the grain. Wipe down the woodwork to remove any dirt or dust. Once dry, paint with two or three coats of emulsion, allowing it to dry between coats.

STEP 2. Cut a strip of fabric to twice the circumference of the bottom of the lampshade by 12cm wide. Fold and stitch a 1cm hem along the bottom edge.

STEP 3. With right sides facing, stitch the short edges of the frill together to form a band. Evenly gather the top edge of this band to make a frill that snugly fits the bottom edge of the lampshade.

STEP 4. Hand sew the frill to the bottom edge of the shade. Cover the top edge of the frill with the ribbon. Pin and hand sew in place to cover any unsightly stitching. For the top edge trim, cut a strip of fabric to the length of the circumference of the top of the lampshade by 5cm wide. Fold and press 1cm hems along both long edges. With right sides facing, stitch the short edges together to form a band. Hand sew in place around the top edge of the lampshade.

STEP 5. For the bow, cut a piece of fabric 30cm x 4cm. With right sides facing, fold in half and stitch short edges together. Turn right side out. Press. Fold the ends into the middle of the bow and tack in place. Make another tube measuring 8cm x 4cm in the same way and fold around the middle of the bow to make a knot. Tack into place. Hand sew bow in position on the top edge of the lampshade.

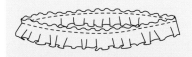

1, 2 & 3. Sand and paint lampstand. Make a frill and gather to fit the bottom edge of the shade.

4. Sew the frill to the bottom edge of the shade, cover the sewn edge with ribbon. Sew other fabric tube to top edge of shade.

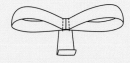

5. Make fabric bow and attach to top edge of shade.

materials

* **Wooden lampstand from junk shop**
* **Newspaper or dustsheet**
* **Medium-grade sandpaper**
* **White emulsion**
* **Large lampshade**
* **Fabric, such as gingham cotton**
* **Sewing thread**
* **Sharp scissors**
* **Ribbon**
* **Lamp carrier**

garden chairs

OLD DIRECTOR'S CHAIRS WITH MOTH-EATEN COVERS CAN BE SMARTENED UP WITH CONTRASTING COTTON AND CANVAS TO MAKE HARD-WEARING SUMMER SEATING.

STEP 1. Make sure the chairs are clean and free from dust. Remove any old nails using pliers.

STEP 2. Cut a piece each of the canvas and the cotton to the size of the chair back plus an extra 00cm for the turn under and 2cm seam allowance all the way around. With right sides together, stitch together the backs on three sides. Turn right side out. Hand sew the opening with small, neat hand stitches to close. Repeat for the chair seat.

STEP 3. Tack the back and seat panels in position on the wooden chair frame using five or six tacks for each side of the material.

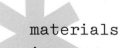

materials

* **Garden chair**
* **Pliers**
* **Tape measure**
* **Fabric, such as heavyweight canvas**
* **Fabric, such as lightweight retro-print cotton**
* **Sewing thread**
* **Upholstery tacks**
* **Hammer**

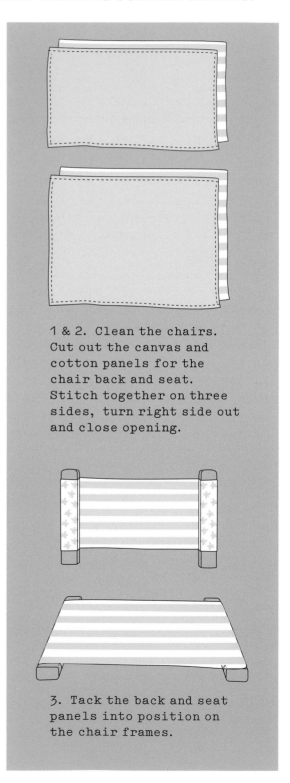

1 & 2. Clean the chairs. Cut out the canvas and cotton panels for the chair back and seat. Stitch together on three sides, turn right side out and close opening.

3. Tack the back and seat panels into position on the chair frames.

retro bag

TURN OFF THE TV AND TURN A CUSHION COVER INTO A SWEET RETRO BAG IN AS LONG AS IT TAKES TO WATCH A COUPLE OF DVDS.

For a neater finish or contrast colour, add a lining to the bag by making a simple sewn 'bag' by hand stitching in place around the top edge.

STEP 1. For the bag handles, cut two 5cm wide strips from across the top edge of the cushion cover, removing the zip.

STEP 2. Cut two pieces of lining fabric to the same size as the fabric strips for the bag handles. Place the handle and lining pieces right sides together and stitch along three sides leaving one end open. Turn right side out. Fold under the raw edge and close the opening by sewing with small neat hand stitches.

STEP 3. For the bag, turn a 1cm double hem to the wrong side all the way around the raw edge of the cushion cover. Pin and stitch.

STEP 4. Pin the handles in place at the top edge of the bag. Attach the handles using reinforced stitching. At each end of the handles, stitch a neat square and stitch across on both diagonals. Repeat by tracing the sewn lines for an extra-secure finish.

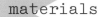

materials

- ✳ Cushion cover, such as retro print cotton
- ✳ Sharp scissors
- ✳ Sewing thread
- ✳ Small remnants of lining fabric

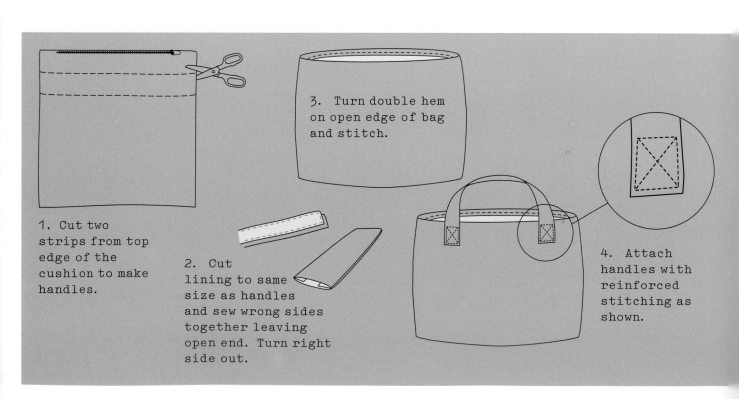

1. Cut two strips from top edge of the cushion to make handles.

2. Cut lining to same size as handles and sew wrong sides together leaving open end. Turn right side out.

3. Turn double hem on open edge of bag and stitch.

4. Attach handles with reinforced stitching as shown.

stockists and suppliers

DIY SUPERSTORES

B&Q
Tel 0845 609 6688
www.diy.com
Everything for the DIYer.

HOMEBASE
Tel 0845 300 1768
www.homebase.co.uk
DIY tools and paints of all kinds.

WICKES
Tel 0870 608 9001
www.wickes.co.uk

FLOORING

ALTERNATIVE FLOORING CO.
Tel 01264 335111
www.alternativeflooring.com

SIESTA CORK TILE CO.
Tel 020 8683 4055
www.siestacorktiles.co.uk
Cork for flooring and walls
available as tiles or on a roll

PAINT

COLE & SON
Tel 020 8442 844
www.cole-and-son.com
Compact range of period colours.

DULUX
Tel 01753 550555
www.dulux.co.uk
Vast collection of paints, including
a heritage range of period colours.

FARROW & BALL
Tel 01202 876141
www.farrow-ball.com
A superb range of paints in
National Trust colours.

JOHN S. OLIVER LTD
Tel 020 7221 6466
www.johnoliver.co.uk

Small range of exotic colours,
including Chinese yellow and
hip pink.

WALLPAPER

B&Q
See under DIY Superstores for
contact details.
Good contemporary geometrics.

COLE & SON
See under Paint for contact
details.
Retro and flock designs.

COLEFAX & FOWLER
Tel 020 7351 0666
Classic English floral prints

FARROW & BALL
See under Paint for contact
details.
Pretty eighteenth-century
inspired florals.

NEISHA CROSLAND
Tel 020 7584 7988
www.neishacrosland.com
Large scale bold prints in
mouth-watering colours.

LOUISE BODY WALLPRINT
Tel 01273 711601
www.louisebodywallprint.com
Beautifully hand-crafted
wallpapers.

OSBOURNE & LITTLE
Tel 020 7352 1456
www.osbourneandlittle.com
Nina Campbell's floral designs
and cotton and upholstery weaves.

PAINT & PAPER LIBRARY
Tel 020 7823 7755
www.paintlibrary.co.uk

WALLPAPERDIRECT
Tel 01323 430886
www.wallpaperdirect.co.uk

A great range of papers and an
excellent price finding service.

FURNITURE

GEORGE SMITH
Tel 020 7384 1004
www.georgesmith.co.uk
Beautiful plump sofas and
chairs in classic shapes.

HABITAT
Tel 0645 334433
www.habitat.net
Modern shapes and colours.

SECOND HAND AND MARKETS

AFTER NOAH
Tel 020 7359 4281
www.afternoah.com
Factory and school-house
furniture and accessories, plus
spun aluminium pendant lights.

ALFIES ANTIQUE MARKET
Tel 020 7723 6066
www.alfiesantiques.com
Everything from sixties furniture
to fabrics, including second-
hand chairs, tables and china.

DECORATIVE LIVING
Tel 020 7736 5623
www.decorativeliving.co.uk
Array of decorative antique
furniture and accessories.

TOBIAS & THE ANGEL
68 White Heart Lane, London
SW13 0PZ
Tel 020 8878 8902
Decorative furniture, metal
watering cans and other
gardening equipment.

BERMONDSEY MARKET
Bermondsey Square, London SE1
(London Bridge underground)

Held early every Friday morning;
antiques plus junk furniture and
accessories.

BRICK LANE MARKET
Brick Lane, London E1
(Liverpool Street underground)
Held every Sunday morning;
junk chairs, tables and
kitchenware.

PORTOBELLO ROAD MARKET
Portobello Road, London W11
(Notting Hill underground)
Held every Friday and Saturday;
sprawling array of stalls selling
antiques and junk furniture and
accessories.

LIGHTING

IKEA
Tel 0845 355 1144
www.ikea.co.uk
Good value contemporary and
classic lamp shades and fittings.

JOHN LEWIS PARTNERSHIP
Tel 020 7730 3434
www.johnlewis.co.uk
Very wide choice of lampbases
and shades.

LAURA ASHLEY
Tel 0870 5622116
www.lauraashley.com
A good range of classic and
traditional lampshades.

SERA OF LONDON
Tel 020 7286 5948
www.seraoflondon.com
Serious lampshades, layers of
silk and chiffon.

FABRICS

DESIGNERS GUILD
Tel 020 7351 5775
www.designersguild.com

Fresh stripes, checks and florals. Sheer organzas, cottons and linen, as well as felt and wool.

IAN MANKIN
Tel 020 7722 0997
Ticking in all colours, plus utility fabrics and good strong canvas useful for garden chairs.

JOHN LEWIS PARTNERSHIP
See Lighting for contact details
Great haberdashery departments with fabrics, ribbons and trimmings. Large selection of dyes, sewing materials and sewing machines.

J.W. BOLLOM & CO LTD
Tel 020 8658 2299
www.bollom.com
Large colour range of flame proof felts (bright pink, blue, green and white are just a few).

LIBERTY
Tel 020 7734 1234
www.liberty.co.uk
Fabulous floral tana lawn cotton.

MACCULLOCH & WALLIS
Tel 020 7629 0311
www.macculloch-wallis.co.uk
A wide range of haberdashery, calico, muslins and gingham.

MELIN TREGWYNT
Tel 01348 891644
www.melintregwynt.co.uk
Checked wool blankets in blues, greens and yellows.

RUSSELL & CHAPPLE
Tel 020 7836 7521
www.randc.net
Canvas, cotton, muslin and linens, both dyed and natural, plus a wonderful green waterproof canvas for outdoors.

THE BUTTON QUEEN
Tel 020 7935 1505
www.thebuttonqueen.co.uk
It's impossible to describe the range of antique and modern buttons stocked here, suffice to say it is diverse enough to suit all requirements.

THE CLOTH SHOP
290 Portobello Road,
London W10 5TE
Tel 020 8968 6001
Everything from winter wools to summer stripes; plenty of natural fibres, such as jute, wool, or silk, all well priced. It also stocks sari silks and antique linen.

V.V. ROULEAUX
Tel 020 7730 3125
www.vvrouleaux.com
Fabulous fuchsia pink and lime green ribbon, plus every sort of trimming imaginable.

HOUSEHOLD LINENS

DESIGNERS GUILD
See Fabrics for contact details
Bold coloured cotton towels.

IKEA
See Lighting for contact details
Good value cotton towels and bathmats. Excellent choice for sheets, pillowcases and duvet covers.

JOHN LEWIS PARTNERSHIP
See Lighting for contact details
Good for cotton towels as well as shower curtains in towelling and canvas.

THE WHITE COMPANY
Tel 0870 900 9555
www.thewhiteco.com
Great plain cotton towels and bedding.

TABLEWARE

THE CONRAN SHOP
Tel 020 7589 7401
www.conran.co.uk
Plain china, blue and white Cornishware and simple glasses.

DAVID MELLOR
Tel 020 7730 4259
www.davidmellordesign.com
Contemporary tableware, glasses and everything for the kitchen.

DIVERTIMENTI
Tel 020 7581 8065
www.divertimenti.co.uk
Good selection of cutlery, china and simple serving dishes.

HABITAT
See Furniture for contact details
Good range of basic china, glasses and cutlery. Brightly coloured cloths and napkins.

IKEA
See Lighting for contact details
Unbeatable value basic china, tumblers and cutlery.

LABOUR & WAIT
Tel 020 7729 6253
www.labourandwait.co.uk
Great utility hardware and enamelled saucepans.

LAKELAND LTD
Tel 015394 88100
www.lakelandlimited.com
All kinds of kitchen tools and other gadgets.

ROBERT WELCH DESIGNS
Tel 01386 840522
www.robertwelch.com
Classic, simple cutlery – my favourite.

WATERFORD WEDGWOOD
Tel 01782 204141
www.wedgwood.com
Simple white dinner plates.

ECO- FRIENDLY

DAMHEAD ORGANIC FOODS,
Tel 0131 448 2091
www.damhead.co.uk.
Eco cleaning products, such as washing-up liquid, bleach and kitchen roll.

ENERGY EFFICIENCY ADVICE CENTRE
Tel 0845 727 7200
www.saveenergy.co.uk

GREEN BUILDING STORE
Tel 01484 854898
www.greenbuildingstore.co.uk

Environmentally friendly loft insulation made from recycled newspapers, non-toxic, solvent-free paints, varnish and stripper.

FURNITURE RECYCLING NETWORK
Tel 01924 375252
www.crn.org.uk
Information about furniture recycling projects.

LAKELAND LTD
See Tableware for contact details
Recycling bird feeder, composting bins, carrier-bag bins, can crushers and airers.

NATURAL COLLECTION
Tel 0870 331 3333
www.naturalcollection.com
Eco-friendly products for all areas of the home by mail order, clockwork radios, organic sheets, clothes airers.

GARDEN

ALLOTMENTS
Allotments are owned by local councils. Find out if there is a waiting list and add your name to it. If there are no allotments in you area contact:
The National Society of Allotment and Leisure Gardeners, O'Dell House, Hunters Road, Corby, Northamptonshire NN17 5JE
Tel 01536 266576
www.nsalg.org.uk
This society suggests that if six people write to the council to ask that they provide allotments, the council will consider the request. They also produce a quarterly magazine for members.

ASSOCIATION KOKOPELLI
Ripple Farm, Crundale, Canterbury, Kent CT4 7EB
www.organicseedsonline.com
Formerly Terre des Semences, a huge selection of organic seeds; varieties of tomatoes, peppers, pumpkins, sunflowers, lavender and alliums.

CHILTERN SEEDS
Tel 01229 581137
www.edirectory.co.uk/chilternseeds
Chiltern Seeds offers, amongst others, the deliciously crunchy red chicory 'Variegata di Castelfranco' and red chicory 'Late Rossa di Chioggia', a bitter leaf that adds bite to salads and looks great.

CROCUS.CO.UK LTD
Tel 01344 629629
www.crocus.co.uk
Varieties of sunflowers, hyacinths, agapanthus, alliums and amaryllis.

DAVID AUSTIN ROSES LTD
Tel 01902 376300
www.davidaustinroses.com
Specialists in English roses, climbers and shrub roses, such as the pink Belle De Crécy, known for its rich fragrance. Also good for ground cover roses and modern shrub roses, including Dapple Dawn, a soft pink rose with a slight musk fragrance.

GARDEN REQUISITES
Tel 01225 851577
www.garden-requisites.co.uk
Arches and arbours, plant trainers and treillage. Inspired by original wirework structures from the nineteenth century.

GROOM BROS LTD
Tel 01775 722421
www.grooms-flowers.co.uk
Good selection of bulbs for autumn and winter planting, including tulips and narcissi.

H. MILES COVENT GARDEN LTD
New Covent Garden Market, London SW8 5NB
Tel 020 7720 7329
Really good for cut flowers, as well as winter-flowering bulbs; they are cheaper when bought by the crate.

HARDY'S COTTAGE GARDEN PLANTS
Tel 01256 896533
www.hardys-plants.co.uk
Specialist in herbaceous perennials; geraniums, irises, delphiniums and foxgloves.

MR FOTHERGILL'S SEEDS
Tel 0845 166 2511
www.mr-fothergills.co.uk
Herb and salad crop seeds, including basil and coriander.

THE ORGANIC GARDENING CATALOGUE
Tel 0845 130 1304
www.organiccatalog.com
Organic fertilisers, pest control solutions, composting bins, and a large choice of seeds including nasturtiums, sunflowers, foxgloves and broad beans.

SUFFOLK HERBS
Tel 01376 572456
www.suffolkherbs.com
Comprehensive range of seeds, including delicious spicy watercress.

FOOD

BRINDISA
Tel 020 7713 1666
www.brindisa.com
Spanish cheeses, olives, chickpeas, olive oil and bottled tomatoes. Jamon from free-range, acorn-fed Black Foot pigs. They run a weekly stall at London's Borough Market.

CARLUCCIO'S
Tel 020 7581 8101
www.carluccios.com
Delicious Italian pasta, cheese and bread. Virgin olive oils and fresh wild mushrooms.

DELL FARM
Painswick, Near Stroud, Gloucestershire GL6 6SQ
Tel 01452 813382
Naturally reared whole or half lambs for the deep freeze.

THE FRESH OLIVE COMPANY
Tel 020 8838 1912
www.fresholive.com
Olives, oils, antipasta and vegetables sourced from Mediterranean family producers.

HENRIETTA GREEN'S FOOD LOVERS BRITAIN
Tel 020 8206 6111
www.foodloversbritain.com
Brainchild of foodie enthusiast, Henrietta Green, who works tirelessly to promote local produce and individual specialist suppliers. Her markets are held all over the country, where you buy real meat from properly reared animals and seasonal fruit and vegetables that taste as they should.

JONES DAIRY
23 Ezra Street, London E2 7RH
Tel 020 7739 5372
www.jonesdairy.co.uk
Old-fashioned food shop selling wonderful English cheeses, homemade cheesecake, freshly ground aromatic coffee and bunches of fresh herbs.

LONDON FARMER'S MARKETS
Tel 020 7704 9659
www.lfm.org.uk
Produce direct from the producers. Homemade cakes, bread, meat fruit and vegetables.

NEAL'S YARD DAIRY
Tel 020 7645 3555
www.nealsyarddairy.co.uk
Excellent British cheeses.

SIERRA RICA
Tel 0034 959 127 327
www.sierrarica.com
Organic foods from Andalucia in Spain, mouth-watering peeled and cooked chestnuts, vegetable spreads, sauces and soups.

STEVE HATT
88–90 Essex Road, London N1
Tel 020 7226 3963
The best fresh wet fish and shellfish. They also have their own smokehouse.

ART SUPPLIERS

CASS ART
Tel 020 7937 6506
www.cassart.co.uk
Paints, brushes, good selection of coloured paper and card. Fabric paints.

GREEN & STONE OF CHELSEA
Tel 020 7352 0837
www.greenandstone.com
Paints and brushes, including specialist art and decorating materials, masking tape and white spirit.

PAPERCHASE
Tel 020 7467 6200
www.paperchase.co.uk
Great selection of coloured papers, funky notebooks and art materials.

WOOLWORTHS
www.woolworths.co.uk
Paint, dyes, sewing materials, plants, seeds and garden kit.

index

acknowledgements

This is my fifth book and, once again, a fabulous team have made it happen. Many, many thanks to: Jenny Zarins for her beautiful pictures and her ace assistant Juliette Cockerill; Lawrence Morton for his witty and smart design, Charlotte Kennedy-Cochran Patrick for her creative endeavours; Melanie Williams, Emma Heath and Tessa Brown for their savvy sewing skills; Kate Storer for more clever illustrations; Alison Cathie, Jane O'Shea, Helen Lewis and Lisa Pendreigh for their support and dedication to my second title with Quadrille; Clare Conville, my wise agent; Tom, Georgia and Grace Brown, Daisy Tudor, Esther-Mei Roditi Yeo; Bea the cat and (the late) Pippi the dog for their modelling talents; Clare and John Riley; David and Katrin Cargill, Tessa Brown and Jonny White, and Mandy Bonnell for kindly letting me use their homes for photography; Colefax & Fowler for the wallpaper on page 45 and Farrow & Ball for wallpaper and paint on page 94.